It Began In An UPPER ROOM

Kenneth D. Barney

Radiant BOOKS

Gospel Publishing House/Springfield, Mo 65802

02-0528

IT BEGAN IN AN UPPER ROOM

Library of Congress Catalog Card Number 78-67445
International Standard Book Number 0-88243-528-0

Printed in the United States of America

Foreword

The format of this book is an alternative to a verse-by-verse or chapter-by-chapter study. It focuses on various aspects of the Early Church's ministry instead of considering events chronologically. As you read you will sweep back and forth through Acts, touching some areas more than once.

There are references in several places to such events as the Day of Pentecost, the healing of the lame man at the temple gate, the food distribution crisis, and the great council meeting. These happenings were so strategic that it is difficult not to mention them in different chapters in this type of approach. You will find the repetition useful as you try to recapture the spiritual atmosphere of those days.

It was my aim to write a study book that is more like a fast-paced story. I felt it necessary to give many Scripture references for the benefit of those who may not have done an extensive study of this portion of the Word before. When the Scripture passages are in Acts, I have given only the chapter and verse, feeling that readers will understand that 2:4 means Acts 2:4, etc. This avoids constant repetition of the word *Acts*.

I hope this book will be enjoyable for those who only want to read rather than study. I also trust it might be useful as a textbook for home Bible-study groups and Sunday school classes. The 13 chapters make it rather practical for a class to study it for one quarter.

Why should Christians today care what Christians did 2,000 years ago? Can the 20th-century church find light and inspiration in the history of the first-century church to guide it through stormy times?

Acts shows us the church in that era closest to the earthly ministry of our Lord Jesus and the outpouring of the Holy Spirit at Pentecost. Its first leaders had been companions of the Saviour day and night for more than 3 years. Several hundred of the original members were with Him after His resurrection. The first martyr beheld Him in His glory after His return to heaven. So did the apostle who arrived on the scene too late to see Him while He was still on earth.

It is not easy for us to grasp what the church was like when those awesome experiences were still fresh to everyone. Fortunately we have the divinely inspired record. On the pages of Acts the Holy Spirit discloses spiritual principles we must never forsake. Some of the props on the stage are different today, and the personnel change often. But the script for the mighty drama is the same, for it has been written by the Head of the Church himself.

KENNETH D. BARNEY

Contents

1

The Story Thus Far

Luke's "Former Treatise"

"The former treatise have I made, O Theophilus, of all that Jesus began both to do and teach" (Acts 1:1).

Luke is referring to his Gospel. Since it is a background for Acts, we should look at it before moving into the story of the Church. In his introduction to Acts, Luke was saying, "My other book tells the story thus far. Here is the way it continues."

As we review events in the latter part of the Gospel of Luke, let's try to imagine we have never read Acts and do not know what is coming. Maybe this will help us appreciate even more what the outpouring of the Holy Spirit meant to the disciples and the future of Christ's work on this earth.

The Last Supper

What a gloomy scene this is if you do not know the rest of the story. The chief priests and scribes were plotting Jesus' death. Their only concern was their uncertainty about public reaction. Now came the thunderbolt: "Then entered Satan into Judas surnamed Iscariot, being of the number of the twelve" (Luke 22:3).

We should have been prepared for this. Judas had shown signs of spiritual deterioration. In fact, there had been reason to wonder how much loyalty he ever had to the Master. But opening the door wide enough for Satan to enter! A man who had been so close to Jesus for so long—how could he do it?

You sense the fiendish glee of Jesus' enemies when Judas approached them. "They were glad." They would reward him financially of course. Judas did not innocently stumble into a trap. He was deliberate and calculating, for "he sought opportunity" to accomplish his treacherous plan. With devilish alertness he watched every move of Jesus.

Other Passovers had been feasts of joy for Jesus and His company, but not this one. Lacking a home of their own, they sought the hospitality of another who would provide them a meeting place. There is deep significance in the words, "And when the hour was come." Yes, it was the hour of the Passover. But it was also the hour that had the attention of the Godhead before Creation. A little while longer and the Lamb of God would be sacrificed on the altar of Calvary.

Try to feel the total outpouring of Jesus' heart as the heavy words came from deep within Him: "With desire I have desired to eat this passover with you before I suffer: for I say unto you, I will not any more eat thereof, until it be fulfilled in the kingdom of God" (22:16).

They always broke bread and drank from the cup at their meals. This time Jesus invested the ordinary routine with an eternal sacredness. From now on it would remind His followers of the breaking of His body and the shedding of His blood.

I think we can be certain none of the disciples understood Jesus' reference to "the new testament."

7

They had lived all of their lives under the old covenant. They were not enlightened yet by the coming of the Spirit. How could they know the old was about to be fulfilled in the new?

The pall of gloom in the Upper Room thickened as Jesus sadly announced that one of them would betray Him. Who could it be? They glanced at one another in horror.

How our Lord's heart ached when the dispute about greatness flared up again among the disciples. Imagine such a question arising at a time like that! *Are you certain, Master, that you didn't make a mistake in choosing this group to carry on Your work?*

Luke does not tell us about Jesus' object lesson of washing the disciples' feet—His obvious answer to their carnal ambitions for prominence. He does record a statement of Jesus that is a guiding principle for every one of us: "He that is greatest among you, let him be as the younger; and he that is chief, as he that doth serve.... I am among you as he that serveth" (22:26, 27).

If you had been one of the Twelve, how would you have reacted when Jesus promised: "And I appoint unto you a kingdom, as my Father hath appointed unto me; that ye may eat and drink at my table in my kingdom, and sit on thrones judging the twelve tribes of Israel"?

They would remember these words often after Pentecost, but now their minds were dull with grief. A kingdom? Jesus must be only trying to lift their spirits. With those hate-filled priests plotting against Him and a betrayer in His own circle, how could He ever have a kingdom?

Satan was after another disciple—Peter. Jesus tried to alert him to the danger while assuring him

8

He had already prayed for him. To Peter's indignant cry that he was ready for imprisonment and martyrdom, Jesus warned that he would deny Him three times before dawn.

Suppose again that you have never read Acts. You have read Jesus' warning to Peter that he is going to fall. But you note he is also destined to have a great ministry. He will be the strengthener of his brethren. He is going to be their leader.

What, you ask yourself, is going to happen to this man to make such a change? Something is! Luke will take up his pen again to tell us about it. Don't miss his next Book.

Gethsemane

The climax to the great drama was approaching. There was a secluded garden where Jesus had gone frequently with His disciples to get away from the crowds. It would soon be a great prayer room in His awful struggle.

The human side of Jesus cried out for support. He could not take His disciples to the place of prayer, for He must wrestle alone with the crushing burden. But he did not leave them far behind—only "a stone's cast."

Look! The men who had been so weighed down with sorrow in the Upper Room were sound asleep when Jesus came back from His hour of agony. These were the leaders of the church He promised to build? the future occupants of thrones?

It was time for the last phase of the conflict. Jesus had already won the victory, but Satan still goaded His enemies to do their worst. It happened just as our Lord had said. Judas directed the mob to the object of their hatred—and he did it with a kiss!

Peter was frantically trying to disprove Jesus' prediction about him. Wildly he swung his sword. His carnal action brought the Master's rebuke. And He restored the ear Peter had severed from a man's head.

Jesus was not taken by surprise. It was all part of the plan known to the Father, Son, and Holy Spirit since the moment sin made its ugly intrusion—and before. It was His adversaries' hour. The power of darkness was allowed to exert its force, but only within divine limitations.

The Cross

The hypocritical religious leaders made a show of conducting a trial. While it was in progress Peter suddenly fell into the devil's sieve. In an unbelievably short time the words of denial escaped his lips three times. Then the rooster crowed and Jesus turned and looked. It was too much for Peter to take. He ran to find a place to sob out his remorse.

This was the man who would strengthen his brethren? Who would strengthen him?

The trial moved from the Sanhedrin to Pilate's court. The chief priests could find Jesus guilty, but they did not have the authority to carry out the death sentence. They encountered a temporary obstacle in Pilate, but the screams of the mob overcame his weak will and he finally cried, "Take Him!"

Never had the death of a man on a cross been like this one. Before it was over one of the thieves executed beside Him called Him "Lord." Somehow he knew the Man on the center cross would have a kingdom. Pitifully, he asked only to be remembered in Jesus' coming moment of triumph.

But the thief's prayer would be answered more gloriously than he dared believe. It was for the redemption of such hopeless men that Jesus came. This is what the Cross is all about. "I will do more than remember you," Jesus assured him. "I will take you with me—today."

For 3 hours before Jesus dismissed His Spirit the sun hid its face. How terrified the priests in the temple must have been as the great veil was suddenly ripped open! It was the day the Passover lamb was killed. But out on the brow of Calvary the real Lamb was crying, "Father, into thy hands I commend my spirit" (23:46).

The Empty Tomb

It was not the Church's future leaders who went to the tomb first. It was a group of devout women. They had to delay their visit because of the Sabbath, but before the first streaks of dawn the following day they were on their way.

It was a blow to them, but today we shout over it: "They found not the body of the Lord Jesus." In a moment two angels brought the announcement that has been the victory song of the Church throughout the centuries: "He is not here, but is risen."

Those dear souls lost no time but hurried to tell the others. Who can read without deep sadness that they reported to "the eleven"? Once there were 12, but Judas struck a bargain with Satan and he never heard the news.

How did the group respond? Luke is blunt about it: "And their words seemed to them as idle tales, and they believed them not." But Peter, still racked by sorrow over his shameful behavior, decided to visit the tomb. He didn't walk; he ran. Apparently he shared the skepticism of the others about the women's report, but what if—?

After Peter saw the deserted tomb and the empty grave clothes he reacted by "wondering."

The pair from Emmaus are typical of all the disciples: "We trusted that it had been he which should have redeemed Israel." Now they were going back to their little village to try to pick up the pieces. In bewilderment they attempted to sort out the stories they had heard. They were especially puzzled about the report of the angels at the tomb who said Jesus was alive.

Luke is the only Gospel writer who records this heartwarming incident. I am glad he shared it with us. This pair so desperately wanted to believe, but they couldn't find a solid reason for faith. Then Jesus caught up with them and walked along, explaining the Scriptures but concealing His identity.

We should note what Luke says about Jesus' exposition of the Word: "And beginning at Moses and all the prophets, he expounded unto them in all the Scriptures the things concerning himself" (24:27). He did not take an isolated text from here and there. He referred to "Moses . . . all the prophets . . . all the Scriptures." Christ's message bears the scrutiny of the whole Word.

The Great Reunion

After Jesus' revelation of himself at the supper table and His sudden disappearance, the Emmaus pair lost no time. They returned to Jerusalem "the same hour," and hurried to the meeting place of the Eleven and the others.

Jesus had already been seen by Peter. It had been a private meeting and is referred to again only in 1 Corinthians 15:5. It is not surprising Jesus met Peter by himself. The big fisherman had failed more miserably than any of the others except Judas. He needed the assurance of Jesus' forgiveness and of his restoration to God's favor.

I can't criticize the disciples' reaction at Jesus' sudden appearance. Can you? "They were terrified and affrighted, and supposed that they had seen a spirit" (Luke 24:37). Nothing like this had happened to them before. It took time for them to adjust to the tremendous events swirling around them.

Just as He did with the disciples from Emmaus, Jesus sought to anchor the hope of all the disciples to the Scriptures:

> These are the words which I spake unto you, while I was yet with you, that all things must be fulfilled, which were written in the law of Moses, and in the prophets, and in the psalms, concerning me. Then opened he their understanding, that they might understand the Scriptures (24:44, 45).

The Great Commission

"And ye are witnesses of these things." This is what the work of the Church is all about. The gospel message is so powerful, yet so simple. Jesus suffered for our sins. He arose from the dead. Remission of sins is available to everyone who repents and believes. This is the truth that must be preached among all nations.

Luke is the only Gospel writer who mentions this statement of Jesus: "And, behold, I send the promise of my Father upon you: but tarry ye in the city of Jerusalem, until ye be endued with power from on high" (24:49). He picks up this theme in the beginning of Acts. It is the thread that connects his Gospel and his second Book.

Luke's description of Christ's ascension is brief,

but spine-tingling. Matthew and John tell us nothing about it, and Mark simply says: "He was received up into heaven" (Mark 16:19). Luke adds these details:

> And he led them out as far as to Bethany, and he lifted up his hands, and blessed them. And it came to pass, while he blessed them, he was parted from them, and carried up into heaven. And they worshipped him, and returned to Jerusalem with great joy: and were continually in the temple, praising and blessing God. Amen (24:50-53).

This is how Luke concludes his "former treatise." He leaves the disciples in the temple. What a happy company they were now. Christ was really going to build His church, and He would use them. He would have a Kingdom and they would be part of it.

The gloom and despair that had saturated the atmosphere of the Upper Room had vanished. Something wonderful would happen very soon. In his second "treatise" Luke will tell us all about it.

2

Blastoff!

The Church's Launching

". . . until the day in which he was taken up" (Acts 1:2).

How many things had awaited the day when He was taken up! The Holy Spirit's new ministry burst on the world only after the Saviour's ascension. The worldwide proclamation of the gospel was stayed until that day. Christ's high-priestly mediation did not begin until He returned to His Father's right hand. His ascension set in motion the forces that will finally crush Satan. How the angels must have made the corridors of heaven ring with hosannas when He was taken up!

The gloom and despair of the hours following their Lord's death were behind the disciples now. The past 40 days had been a foretaste of heaven. The little band had seen many infallible proofs that this was indeed the same Jesus who had once been dead.

We are not told all the commandments Jesus gave His followers. Luke does not list all "the things pertaining to the kingdom of God" of which He spoke. But we can be sure the Holy Spirit brought everything back to their memories in the days that followed.

15

Those men and women were commissioned to take the message of redemption to the whole world. But not yet. First they must wait.

We sometimes think waiting is a sin. Yet there are times when it is the only thing to do if we would be at our best for God. Activity should not always have priority.

The Coming Baptism

The disciples' waiting was for a special purpose— the fulfillment of "the promise of the Father." Jesus reminded them He had already told them of this promise before. The coming of the Holy Spirit had been uppermost in His conversations with them during the tense hours before His arrest. They had been too sad to comprehend the message then. How fully they understood it now we cannot be sure. But Jesus told them to wait, and so they did.

These folks knew something of the Holy Spirit's ministry from the Old Testament. But a baptism in the Spirit was something new. To help them grasp it Jesus spoke of John's water baptism. Many of them had seen the rugged prophet plunge repentant sinners into the Jordan. How completely submerged they were; how saturated with the water in which they were immersed.

"For John truly baptized with water; but ye shall be baptized with the Holy Ghost not many days hence" (1:5). What a picture! A new age was about to arrive when the risen Christ would plunge cleansed believers into the depths of His Spirit as John had baptized Israelites in the river. Jesus assured His little company the waiting would not be long. The Baptism would come "not many days hence."

Final Instructions

But those dear souls were still fervent Jews. They were as weary of Caesar's rule as anyone. They had not shaken off the belief that the Messiah's mission was to smash Rome and occupy David's throne. Their question was sincere. Spiritually they were like kindergarten pupils. "Lord, wilt thou at this time restore again the kingdom to Israel?"

They were believers, but their vision extended only as far as their own nation. This was one of the misconceptions from which their Lord must free them. They did not discern His burden for the whole world. Nor did they grasp the spiritual character of His kingdom during this age.

Jesus' answer was a good one for Christians of all times: "It is not for you to know." We are full of curiosity. If we had our way, God would reveal the whole future to us. We want everything spelled out in detail *now*. But the life of faith demands that some things be committed to God. The "times and seasons" are in His power. We have our hands full doing God's real work without trying to delve into all the side issues.

The vital thing, Jesus declared, is that His followers would receive power. He was speaking of a clothing of supernatural energy. This power is "heavenly dynamite." There were forces more tenacious than Rome out in the Satan-dominated world. They were spiritual forces and must be fought with spiritual power. No one has such strength in himself. But when the Holy Spirit comes, what a difference!

Above all, the power of the Spirit makes witnesses of God's people. This truth may sound too simple. We are interested in bigger things, but this is how

Jesus chose to build His church. Each one cleansed by His blood will become a witness to others still in the clutches of sin. For that witnessing we must have power. Not psychological power, arguing power, or intellectual power, but power from "on high."

How is a jury convinced in a courtroom trial? By witnesses who have firsthand evidence to offer. The world will be convinced of the reality of Christ as His Spirit-filled witnesses show evidence that being a Christian makes a difference.

Finally the separation came. Jesus had completed His earthly work, including His postresurrection ministry. The disciples wanted to keep Him forever, but this could not be. "And when he had spoken these things, while they beheld, he was taken up; and a cloud received him out of their sight" (1:9).

Significant words: "Out of their sight." The new age was at hand. They would walk by faith now. Yet it would not be blind faith. They were not spiritual orphans. The other Comforter was coming soon. He would guide them into all truth.

> And while they looked steadfastly toward heaven as he went up, behold, two men stood by them in white apparel; which also said, Ye men of Galilee, why stand ye gazing up into heaven? this same Jesus, which is taken up from you into heaven, shall so come in like manner as ye have seen him go into heaven (1:10, 11).

"This same Jesus . . . shall so come." How wonderful that the angels quickly announced the Church's blessed hope. We are not permitted to speculate about the day or hour, but Jesus himself told us the signs that will signal His return. When the moment comes, that glorious One splitting the skies will be the "same Jesus" who was received back to heaven.

Back to the Upper Room

The distance from the Mount of Olives to Jerusalem is short. Who can doubt that those radiant souls traveled it with springing step and joyful song? What a difference in their walk now and the way they had stolen through the streets seeking a hiding place after Jesus' death!

Life now had an electrifying purpose. They were waiting for something—something tremendous, new, and revolutionary—the promise of the Father; the baptism in the Holy Spirit. It would not be long. A glorious new dispensation was only a few days away.

Waiting time need not be dull. It can be exciting and profitable. For those disciples there were no hours for idle chatter. They "continued with one accord in prayer and supplication." Both men and women were in the group. The remaining 11 apostles were present. The New Testament's last reference to Jesus' mother, Mary, tells us she was also there. So were His brothers—once sarcastic unbelievers.

Church business meetings are not always noted for their spiritual tone. But this one was. In his usual role as leader, Peter stood up to remind his companions that something important must be attended to. They realized Judas' tragic betrayal had been a fulfillment of Scripture, but this vacancy in their ranks must not remain.

The little company took care of the matter in the only way they knew. They resorted to the ancient practice of casting lots. It might be compared to our drawing of straws or picking a name out of a hat. They are to be commended for praying first and not considering the lot-casting a matter of mere chance.

They wanted God's man to fill Judas' place. I have no doubt that God honored their simple trust. Matthias was chosen. Now there were 12 again instead of 11.

After Pentecost we have no record of the church casting lots. On this occasion God helped them in spite of their immaturity. One thing the Spirit does, however, is to guide us away from practices that belong to spiritual babyhood. Putting out fleeces, closing our eyes while putting a finger on a random Bible verse, or other games of spiritual roulette should be shunned. For people who have the Scriptures and the indwelling Spirit, such things are childish. They also are too closely connected with superstition.

On Schedule

The disciples did not have to wait 10 days to persuade God to send His Spirit. He moves on schedule, and He would launch the Church on the day of the Jewish Feast of Weeks. In the New Testament it is called Pentecost.

Centuries before Jesus died, it was ordained in the counsels of the Godhead that His death should occur at Passover. It could not have happened on any other day because the Passover lamb was a type of Jesus.

The Feast of Weeks was a harvest celebration. How fitting that the spiritual harvest of the Church Age should commence at such a time! The appointed day must "fully come." This is why the disciples had to wait, although they were not aware of the divine arrangement.

Never overlook the disciples' faithfulness in preparing their hearts for the Spirit. They remained "in one place." No one deserted his post. Best of all, they stayed "in one accord." How difficult we make the

Spirit's work when we permit discord and division. How many places of responsibility are vacated by Christians who become weary in well doing. It was different with those people. Like the Israelites of old, they made the valley full of ditches to prepare for God's visitation.

The Holy Spirit—the Bible's real Author—wanted us to know the tornadic sound that filled the Upper Room was from heaven. We have heard all kinds of sounds from earth, but few from heaven. It was not so on that day in Jerusalem. God spoke. His mighty wind invaded a place of prayer. Not a corner was missed. The record says the wind filled the whole house.

The presence of God filled the whole building, and this is what He wants to do in our churches today. How refreshing to watch the flesh stand back in speechless wonder as God sweeps in!

There was fire too—a different kind of fire. Not a single blaze, but individual flames in the shape of tongues that hovered over every waiting believer.

All of these supernatural manifestations confirmed one fact—the coming of the Spirit of God. "They were all filled with the Holy Ghost" (2:4). Luke does not use many words to describe this stupendous event. They aren't needed; the picture is clear.

Wind and fire were not new symbols of God's presence. In the Old Testament He often revealed himself by fire. Who can forget the whirlwind that took Elijah to heaven?

A New Sign

But a new sign appeared now. Each one of the 120 opened his mouth and began to speak, but not in his own language. They all poured out their adoration of the Lord in other tongues. Through human lips the Spirit himself declared the wonderful works of God. This had not happened before. A new age had suddenly exploded on the world, accompanied by a new sign.

What could be more fitting than the sign of other tongues? Is any part of our body more treacherous than the tongue? James says it is our most unruly member; full of deadly poison (James 3:8).

In the Upper Room the Spirit of God took such control of His people that the languages they spoke were His choosing. It was a testimony that during the new age the Spirit would be *in* God's people, not merely with them. Redeemed humans would be His temples. He would make His home in cleansed lives. To introduce this miraculous change of dispensations, the Spirit took command of the whole being of each disciple. The little congregation did not know the languages in which they spoke, but the Spirit did. It was He who directed their flow of praise in other tongues.

Multitudes were in the city for the feasts. Christ did not begin to build His church in secret. The mighty work of Pentecost was not done in a corner. Jews had gathered from many nations. They were devout men, the record says. Devout, but not saved.

Just how the report of the events was "noised abroad" we are not told. But when God shows His power it does not take long for the word to spread. Fire attracts a crowd, and news of the fire blazing in the Upper Room sent thousands to the scene. Now the disciples were in the streets. A few weeks ago they had been hiding in fear. Now they were celebrating openly the resurrection of their Lord.

"What Meaneth This?"

The crowd was stunned by the phenomenon of Galileans extolling God in foreign languages. The people were full of questions; for the most part they were honest ones. Modern church services do not often cause people to be amazed and marvel. Not many today are "confounded" by what they see and hear in the religious world. It was different at Pentecost. The puzzled crowd sought an answer. "What meaneth this?" was the question on everyone's lips.

A few tried to dismiss the whole affair by declaring that they were just a bunch of drunks celebrating. It is doubtful anyone took this seriously. There was too much electricity in the air to be explained so frivolously.

Note the significance of these statements: "Because that every man heard them speak in his own language. . . . We do hear them speak in our tongues the wonderful works of God" (2:6, 11). There were people present who spoke various languages, but everyone heard and understood the message. The gospel is for all men, all tongues, all languages, and all races.

When men sincerely seek an answer to what God is doing, He will respond. The Holy Spirit gave Peter a word of knowledge straight from the Scriptures. Suddenly the apostle knew "this is that." Joel's ancient prophecy was being fulfilled before their eyes (Joel 2:28-32). Peter's audience knew that prophecy. The Holy Spirit quickened it in Peter's mouth and in their hearts. Three thousand were convicted of sin, righteousness, and judgment! The Spirit was doing what Jesus said He would do when He came. Jerusalem soon witnessed a gigantic baptismal service.

We sometimes hear of amazing church growth, but have you ever witnessed a church's membership jumping from 120 to 3,120 in one day? It happened that day. The Spirit had come! The disciples were endued with power from on high.

Peter's message at Pentecost was a masterpiece of powerful simplicity. This was not because he had skillfully planned it. It was completely extemporaneous. He was a witness. Like his fellow believers he was a Spirit-filled proclaimer of the truth that Jesus had died and risen again. Didn't our Lord promise the Holy Spirit would testify of Him? Nothing proved this more than Peter's sermon. Its whole theme was Jesus.

The New Age

The Day of Pentecost was the beginning, not the end. The believers did not disband and cherish a memory. They continued steadfastly in the apostles' doctrine and fellowship (2:42). They prayed together every day. They worshiped. They testified. They filled Jerusalem with the doctrine of Christ.

We are told in Acts 2:43 that "fear came upon every soul." The atmosphere was not raucous, coarse, or frivolous. A profound reverence overshadowed the church. Everyone walked as though he were on holy ground.

For a time, the church coped with the emergency of having many extra people in their midst without funds by pooling their resources and living from a common treasury. This was not permanent. It was a measure adopted to meet a unique and temporary need.

Undoubtedly, it would take volumes to record the story of the weeks that followed Pentecost. The Holy

Spirit tells it simply and beautifully in the closing words of the second chapter:

> And they, continuing daily with one accord in the temple, and breaking bread from house to house, did eat their meat with gladness and singleness of heart, praising God, and having favor with all the people. And the Lord added to the church daily such as should be saved (vv. 46, 47).

3

The Hovering Cloud

The Influence of the Holy Spirit
in the Early Church

Mark concluded his Gospel with these dramatic words:

> So then, after the Lord had spoken unto them, he was received up into heaven, and sat on the right hand of God. And they went forth, and preached every where, the Lord working with them, and confirming the word with signs following. Amen (Mark 16:19, 20).

Mark does not say, "The Lord worked," or, "The disciples worked." He says they worked *together*. "The Lord working with them" is the theme of the Acts story. It began when Christ returned to heaven. It received its powerful thrust forward when He sent the Spirit to launch the Church. Like the cloud that hovered constantly over Israel in the wilderness, the Spirit of God overshadowed the Early Church day and night. Without Him there would have been no Book of Acts to write.

The first mention of the Spirit in Acts is in 1:2. It concerns our Lord Jesus. Luke says it was through the Holy Ghost that He gave commandments to the apostles. Everything our Saviour did while He was

26

in the flesh was by the strength and grace of the Spirit within Him.

The fire and the rushing, mighty wind at Pentecost symbolized a Personality who cannot be limited or controlled by the mere will of man. It is a dangerous travesty for anyone to try to manipulate the Spirit of God. We do not strive for more of Him. He must have more of us.

One of the clear marks of the early Christians was the desire of each one to use his experience for the work of the Lord and not for personal blessing. The outward signs accompanying the Spirit's descent excited the crowd, but they were not the most vital part of the disciples' experience. It was what remained after the wind and fire vanished that propelled the Church onward. There was a new stability among the disciples after Pentecost. Their fellowship was deepened. They realized they were a body, not a mob of individuals. The new spirit of prayer and worship after the Spirit's coming was beautiful.

"Not Drunken"

Peter lost no time in answering the charge that the disciples had had too much wine. "These are not drunken, as ye suppose" (2:15). The verdict of the critics was wrong, but it did point out the startling change in the disciples' behavior. If there is no difference in the way a Christian lives after he is filled with the Spirit, there is reason to wonder what kind of experience he had. The Holy Spirit makes a change.

In his altar call at Pentecost, Peter made the reception of the Spirit a vital matter: "Repent, and be baptized every one of you in the name of Jesus Christ for the remission of sins, and ye shall receive the gift of the Holy Ghost" (2:38). Too often this emphasis has been missing from the church's message. Sinners not only need to be saved from their sins, but also empowered by the Spirit after their salvation to make them effective witnesses for Christ.

Peter assures us: "The promise is unto . . . as many as the Lord our God shall call" (2:39). Some theologians remind me of a man who has a mansion but has furnished only one room while the rest are bare. There are those who would shut up the great blessing of the Holy Spirit within that era called the Apostolic Age. Jesus said nothing to suggest that what happened to the Early Church was their exclusive experience. The ministry of the Spirit continues throughout this age. It will not be completed until the Church is raptured and "that great and notable day of the Lord come" (2:20).

When Peter and the others were arrested, Peter's testimony to the religious leaders told the story of Pentecost so forcefully: "And we are his witnesses of these things; and so is also the Holy Ghost, whom God hath given to them that obey him" (5:32).

The testimony of Spirit-filled Christians is different from that of ordinary witnesses. The disciples did not speak in their own unaided strength. There was an added force to their words. Their witness was set aflame by the Holy Spirit. The cloud hovered over the growing company. God and man were working together.

Peter connects the reception of the Spirit with obedience: ". . . the Holy Ghost, whom God hath given to them that *obey* him." How many Christians lack the Spirit's power because of disobedience in some area of their lives? Only God can know, but it is a serious question. When the Spirit moved through the Church, as we read in Acts, it was because God's people were obedient. They strained their spiritual ears for the Lord's voice. When they heard Him they were quick to respond.

Peter's testimony had a powerful effect: "When they heard that, they were cut to the heart, and took counsel to slay them" (5:33). The Greek word for "cut" means "sawn in two." This was the effect of the Spirit's convicting power. These stubborn, wicked people felt their hearts had been sawn in two. This should help us realize what it means for men to deal with the Spirit of God. Christians can be encouraged to know the Spirit is working with them in their soul-winning ministry.

The Fire Scatters

Many Christians were driven from their homes by persecution, but instead of being cowed they went everywhere preaching the Word (8:4). If we could read the record of each one, it would keep us shouting for a long time. We do have the account of one—Philip, a deacon. The Lord led him to Samaria. There was an immediate response to his ministry: multitudes were saved, sick bodies were healed, and demons were cast out. A sorcerer named Simon, who had held the city in his grip, professed salvation. The miracles and signs he saw caused him to "wonder" (8:13).

Then Peter and John came from Jerusalem to pray for the new converts to receive the Holy Spirit. The Lord saw fit to give us no details of this outpouring except these: "Then laid they their hands on them, and they received the Holy Ghost" (8:17).

But as brief as this account is, it indicates that something even more startling than the miracles took place at that moment. Simon had not offered to

29

buy Philip's evangelistic zeal or his gifts of healing, miracles, and faith. Yet when he saw new Christians being filled with the Spirit he was overwhelmed. "Give me also this power," he cried.

We are told in verse 18 that Simon "saw" something when the Spirit came on the Samaritans. The Scriptures do not say what it was, but obviously it was conspicuous and exciting.

Philip had been in the Upper Room and had witnessed the sign of other tongues. So had Peter and John, who came to pray for the new congregation. Is there any reason to doubt they saw this Pentecostal sign repeated at Samaria?

Simon's error should be a warning to all of us. It is a serious thing to want the Holy Spirit simply to give us power to do something spectacular. It is much more important that we be concerned with what the Spirit can do inside of us. This is the theme of 1 Corinthians 13.

When Philip left Samaria at the Lord's command, he was led out into the desert where a chariot had stopped. In it a man sat reading from a scroll of Scripture. He was the secretary of the treasury of Ethiopia. "Then Philip opened his mouth, and began at the same Scripture, and preached unto him Jesus" (8:35).

Throughout the Book of Acts you will notice the Christians' complete reliance on the Word. The Spirit never works apart from it. Never.

The Arrester Arrested

The great turning point in the Acts story came with the conversion of Saul. As he waited, blinded, in Damascus, God sent to him a disciple named

Ananias. Ananias' attitude toward this man whose hostility he had once feared is beautiful:

> And Ananias went his way, and entered into the house; and putting his hands on him said, Brother Saul, the Lord, even Jesus, that appeared unto thee in the way as thou camest, hath sent me, that thou mightest receive thy sight, and be filled with the Holy Ghost (9:17).

Saul had already accepted Christ. Two more miracles were in store for him—the healing of his eyes and the infilling of the Spirit. Being filled with the Spirit was such a natural outcome of salvation in those days that there was never any thought of disconnecting the two experiences. Ananias mentioned Paul's healing and his baptism in the Spirit in the same breath.

Great things happened in the Church following Saul's conversion: "Then had the churches rest throughout all Judea and Galilee and Samaria, and were edified; and walking in the fear of the Lord, and in the comfort of the Holy Ghost, were multiplied" (9:31).

Did you notice the order here? The fear of the Lord is mentioned first, for there is a close connection between it and the comfort of the Holy Ghost. A light, frivolous spirit never prepares the heart for the Spirit's inward work. The fear of the Lord and the comfort of the Holy Ghost were not something those disciples experienced spasmodically. They "walked" in this spirit consistently.

The Spirit's leadership and the Christians' joyful submission to it is a theme that dominates the Acts record. The other Comforter had taken command of the Church. His power and influence were never absent. We are reading the Acts of the *Holy Spirit* when we open this "fifth Gospel."

A Vision and a Trip

Until chapter 10 the church was Jewish. God works in His own time, and now it was the hour for another crisis. It took a vision to convince a faithful Jew like Peter he should go to a Gentile home.

Again the Spirit took command. Despite his prejudices, Peter was sensitive to the Spirit. As he was in deep thought about his vision, "the Spirit said unto him, Behold, three men seek thee. Arise therefore, and get thee down, and go with them, doubting nothing: for *I have sent them*" (10:19, 20). The Spirit was working on both ends of the situation.

Any preacher would like to face a congregation like the one that greeted Peter in Cornelius' house. He did not have to go out and round them up. They were waiting eagerly to hear what he had to tell them: "How God anointed Jesus of Nazareth with the Holy Ghost and with power: who went about doing good, and healing all that were oppressed of the devil; for God was with him" (v. 38).

According to the record, Peter said nothing in his simple message about the baptism in the Holy Spirit. But he lifted up Jesus, and in this the Spirit delights. Verses 44 and 45 record the Gentile Pentecost:

> While Peter yet spake these words, the Holy Ghost fell on all them which heard the word. And they of the circumcision which believed were astonished, as many as came with Peter, because that on the Gentiles also was poured out the gift of the Holy Ghost.

How did Peter and His Jewish companions know the Spirit had fallen on the Gentiles? There was the same sign that had appeared when they were filled in the Upper Room: "For they heard them speak with tongues, and magnify God" (v. 46).

That settled it! If any of Peter's old feelings remained, they vanished quickly. There was no doubt about it. God had opened the door to the Gentiles. The Spirit bore witness to that.

But the story was not over. Not everyone was happy about this apostolic visit to the Gentiles. Chapter 11 records a confrontation: "And when Peter was come up to Jerusalem, they that were of the circumcision contended with him, saying, Thou wentest in to men uncircumcised, and didst eat with them" (vv. 2, 3).

Peter had no trouble giving his answer. He had gone to Cornelius' house at the direction of the Spirit, as he declared in verse 12. And the clincher was: "The Holy Ghost fell on them, as on us at the beginning" (v. 15). How could Peter forget that "beginning," even though about 10 years had passed? His memory of Pentecost was as vivid as his memory of his Lord's resurrection. When a church forgets the Spirit's ministry, decline and decay aren't far away.

Commissioned by the Spirit

Who called the first missionaries? Who drew men out of the company of a thriving congregation and sent them to the regions where Jesus' name had never been declared? "As they ministered to the Lord, and fasted, the Holy Ghost said, Separate me Barnabas and Saul for the work whereunto I have called them" (Acts 13:2).

How heartening it is when men who labor for God know they are not marching under their own orders. Stern tests lay ahead for those preachers, but they had a mandate from the Spirit. Christians like that are hard to stop. Prisons, shipwrecks, wild beasts, and bloodthirsty mobs have difficulty handling men who have such a commission burning in their bones.

Verses 3 and 4 demonstrate the beautiful cooperation of believers and the Spirit: "And when they had fasted and prayed, and laid their hands on them, they sent them away. So they, being sent forth by the Holy Ghost, departed unto Seleucia; and from thence they sailed to Cyprus."

First the record says "they" sent them away. Then it says they were "sent forth by the Holy Ghost." Both statements were wonderfully true. Christians who were sensitive to the Spirit were His instruments in launching the church's first missionary program. The Spirit and men were working together.

A Council and a Letter

The great council meeting of Acts 15 will be discussed more fully in another chapter. We will pause long enough here to note the contents of the letter sent to the Gentile churches after the meeting. It began with these words: "For *it seemed good to the Holy Ghost, and to us*, to lay upon you no greater burden than these necessary things" (15:28).

Those Christians had things in the right order. It is easy to become so carnal that we are chiefly concerned over what seems good to us. It was not so with that earnest company. What pleased the Holy Spirit came first. When they discovered what seemed good to Him, it immediately became good to them.

Peter's great point of emphasis during the council was that God had given the Holy Spirit to the Gentiles just as He had to the Jewish believers (15:8). The gift of the Spirit to men and women is God's testimony that they are His. In spite of their misgiv-

34

ings, the Jewish Christians in the meeting were impressed by the outpouring of the Spirit on the Gentiles. In the final analysis this was what melted their resistance.

The Divine Superintendent

Whose book can do justice to the subject of the Spirit's activity in the Early Church? Acts is church history, but we will miss the whole point of that history if we fail to recognize that it is a record of the Spirit of God indwelling and working through human beings. Not just any human beings, of course, but those cleansed by the blood of Jesus.

We will refrain from dealing at length with some examples of the Spirit's activities in Acts because we will speak of them later. But we would remind our readers that it was to the Holy Spirit that Peter said Ananias and Sapphira lied (5:3, 9). The Spirit caught away Philip after he led the eunuch to Christ (8:39). It was by the Spirit that Agabus warned the church of a coming famine (11:28). The Spirit checked Paul and Barnabas on certain occasions and turned them westward (16:6, 7, 9). Paul said the Holy Spirit sets leaders over churches (20:28). And it was by the Spirit that the apostle was warned of his coming troubles (21:10, 11).

"It seemed good to the Holy Ghost, and to us" (15:28). There should be no different spirit in the church in any age.

4

Hot Line to Heaven

The Early Church's Prayer Life

As life moves on we sometimes have a tendency to ignore the basics. Sooner or later, however, we come to a place where we realize that we dare not become dislodged from the foundation on which we began.

Prayer is one of the basics of Christian living. It is easy to take a "ho-hum" attitude when someone talks or writes about it. We have heard about prayer so much, and agree that it is important, but other subjects seem more exciting. The truth is if you want exciting things to happen, prayer must happen first.

The prayer life of the Early Church was the power plant that made it go. The Acts story should correct any notion we might have that after being filled with the Spirit we can finally relax in our praying. The term "praying through" is familiar to us, but at times it seems to take on unfortunate connotations. Some people pray until they are filled, and then they are "through" for all time to come!

Not so with that company in the Upper Room. What started there never stopped. Acts 2:42 mentions four things that "continued steadfastly" after Pentecost: doctrine, fellowship, breaking of bread, and prayer.

How the coming of the Spirit enriched all these areas of church life! Prayer took on new dimensions. The Spirit of God now made His home in every believer as a permanent resident. When they did not know how to pray, the Spirit himself made intercession for them, as Paul later taught He would do (Romans 8:26, 27).

Jesus' own example left its mark on the disciples. When they slipped up to His private prayer spot one day and listened to Him, they were so impressed that they cried, "Lord, teach us to pray" (Luke 11:1). They knew He often left His bed while they still slept to find a place of communion with His Father. They were aware of the nights He did not go to bed at all because He had to pray. With what awe they must have listened to His great high-priestly prayer just before the Cross (John 17).

Familiarity with prayer had not bred contempt in these people. Receiving the baptism in the Holy Spirit intensified their thirst for communion with their God.

3 p.m. and Time for Prayer

Let's move from the second chapter to the third. The Day of Pentecost had past. The church was growing every day. Revival was in the air. But no one had forgotten the basics. Acts 3:1 records the simple statement: "Now Peter and John went up together into the temple at the hour of prayer, being the ninth hour."

I think we can conclude from the wording that this was something these men did regularly. They were Christians, but they were also Jews who were accustomed to observing set times of prayer. If this had become mere routine with them in the past, it certainly was not since the coming of the Spirit.

I like the expression "went up together." There were no loners in that group. When God's people get together in their devotions and prayer, the stage is set for the Lord to work. And work He did on that day! Before the two apostles ever got to the prayer meeting a lame beggar at the gate was healed in the name of Jesus. Great things can happen when we are on our way to keep an appointment at the Throne.

The crowd that had gathered for 3 p.m. prayers suddenly found themselves witnesses to a miracle. Things like this had not been happening in the temple. Their prayer meetings weren't usually interrupted by healed people leaping in the air and shouting spontaneous praises! But something new had hit Jerusalem. Men and women were being saved daily and filled with the Spirit of God. They were in touch with the Lord, and He was in touch with them. These disciples of Jesus were like wires through which the electricity of heaven flowed, and their prayer life kept the power turned on.

The healing of the lame man aroused the hostility of the Jewish leaders, who promptly put Peter and John in jail (4:1-3). Of course, the disciples returned immediately to their own company when they were freed. What followed seems to have been the normal, spontaneous activity of the church. They started to pray. No one had to spend 15 minutes trying to "pump" things up. Prayer burst out of them like an oil field gusher.

One Voice

"And when they heard that, they lifted up their voice to God with one accord" (4:24). The record

38

does not say "voices," but "voice." When God listens to us does He hear a multitude of voices, or one voice? That voice was "with one accord." Verse 32 says they were of "one heart and . . . one soul." No wonder the place was shaken! Could it be this is why the church isn't shaking many things today—there are many voices instead of one voice?

They didn't ask God to stop the persecution or make things easier for them. They only asked for more boldness to proclaim the Word. They prayed for God to confirm their witness with signs and wonders that everyone would recognize as being done in the name of Jesus.

God answered. He will always answer prayers of that kind. Their petition for more boldness was granted. The believers were filled again with the Spirit. Verse 33 describes the results: "And with great power gave the apostles witness of the resurrection of the Lord Jesus: and great grace was upon them all." Great praying followed by great grace! This is God's order. You can't enjoy great grace any other way.

The atmosphere of the church was affected by this mighty season of prayer. Their fellowship and concern for one another were deepened:

> Neither was there any among them that lacked: for as many as were possessors of lands or houses sold them, and brought the prices of the things that were sold, and laid them down at the apostles' feet: and distribution was made unto every man according as he had need (4:34, 35).

First Things First

We will discuss the food-distribution problem (Acts 6) in more detail later. But we must note here the reason the apostles wanted someone else to assume this burden was to keep themselves unencumbered by matters that would hinder their prayer life and their ministry of the Word (6:4).

Those Spirit-filled men were wise enough to know that if they sacrificed their prayer time the Church would suffer. It is one of Satan's tricks to tie the hands of Christ's ministers with so many worthwhile projects that they cannot give priority to what should have it—prayer and the ministry of the Word. Thank God for spiritual leaders who are determined this will not happen. God will bless congregations who are spiritually sensitive enough to recognize the divine order.

When seven men were chosen for the necessary work of caring for the widows, they did not begin their task until the apostles had prayed for them (6:6). Nothing was done without talking to the Lord about it. Prayer can become a form and a lifeless ritual if the Spirit's touch is not maintained. But His rich anointing permeated every prayer meeting in those days and kept the Church alive and powerful and able to meet any challenge that arose.

The first Christian martyr, Stephen, left the world with a prayer on his lips. It was the same kind his Saviour had prayed on the cross: "Lord, lay not this sin to their charge" (7:60). Such words don't spring from one who calls on the Lord only in emergencies. The touch of the Spirit on Stephen's life was so unbroken that this cry of forgiveness was simply the outgrowth of a praying heart.

Before Peter and John laid their hands on the new converts at Samaria so they might receive the Holy Spirit, they prayed (8:15). They were not so presumptuous as to believe the outpouring of the Spirit would happen automatically with the imposition of their hands. They would not take the step until they had made contact with the Head of the Church.

Simon the Sorcerer, even with evil still in his heart, saw such power in the prayer life of Peter that he implored the apostle, "Pray ye to the Lord for me," after Peter had warned him where he was heading (8:24).

What was the blinded Saul doing when God called Ananias to go to the house on Straight Street and minister to him? He was praying (9:11). I think we can safely assume he was not engaging in the lifeless prayer forms of his old religion. He had met the risen Christ, and prayer was already becoming as spontaneous as breathing.

Even though Peter had witnessed previous miracles, he did not assume he could see Tabitha raised from the dead without praying. What boldness it would take to face a corpse and say, "Arise." Peter did not do it without first clearing the room of spectators and falling on his knees in prayer (9:40).

How did the Gentile Cornelius finally realize the deep longings of his heart for the real knowledge of God? Even before he heard the message of Christ he had sought the Lord earnestly in prayer, for the angel told him, "Thy prayers and thine alms are come up for a memorial before God" (10:4). Peter got the message from heaven to go to Cornelius' house when he went to the housetop in Joppa to pray (10:9).

Prayer and an Iron Gate

The church had seasons of both peace and trouble. Wicked Herod sought favor with the Jews by unleashing his murderous wrath on the Christians. James the brother of John was his first victim, and Peter was intended as his second. "And when he had apprehended him, he put him in prison, and delivered him to four quaternions of soldiers to keep him; intending after Easter to bring him forth to the people" (12:4).

This was what Herod intended to do. What was to stop him? He had the authority and he was cruel enough to shed blood without a twinge of conscience. But elsewhere in the city something was going on that would overrule the intentions of this godless ruler. "Prayer was made without ceasing of the church unto God for him" (v. 5). How many times the plans of men have been changed by prayer!

Peter did spend some time in chains. He was not delivered the first day. He had been the channel through which God worked miracles. He had prayed the prayer of faith many times. Yet when this crisis arose he did not cause the chains to fall from his own hands or make the iron prison gate open. He had to depend on the prayers of others.

We never arrive at the place in our Christian lives where this is not true. God does answer individual prayers, but He also works through the united prayers of the Church. Perhaps this is to keep us aware that we are part of a body. We need one another; we cannot make it alone. What a comfort it is when a brother or sister in Christ puts a hand on our shoulder during a time of great need and says quietly, "I'm praying for you."

This must have been a nonstop, round-the-clock prayer meeting. When Peter was delivered by the angel during the night hours, he went immediately to Mark's mother's house "where many were gathered together praying" (12:12). Did you notice that despite the late hour there were still "many" on their knees? You can't stop a church like that. Herod had something on his hands that was beyond his control. The people he was trying to drive out of business were a group that kept the hot line to heaven open 24 hours a day.

We have often heard this account discussed with amusement because the people who were praying for Peter's deliverance would not believe he was really at the door. But who are we to smile at this? Have we not sometimes been surprised when God answered our prayers? Despite this evidence that they were still very human, there had been enough real faith in the prayers that rocketed heavenward to bring the angel of the Lord to the scene. Prayer snapped a prisoner's chains and swung open an iron gate.

Prayer at All Seasons

What a congregation there was at Antioch; what a collection of spiritual leaders! No wonder it was the church from which the Holy Spirit launched the first apostolic missionary offensive.

It is evident that prayer had priority in Antioch, for it was while "they ministered to the Lord, and fasted" that the Spirit of God called Barnabas and Saul (13:2). They lost no time in answering, but they did not leave until the church had fasted and prayed and laid their hands on them (v. 3). You can sense a cloud of prayer hovering over that church like the cloud of incense that covered the altar in the tabernacle.

When Paul and Silas answered God's call to Macedonia and found themselves in stocks in the city jail, they responded with the Christian's secret weapon. At the dark hour of midnight they could contain their joy no longer, and began to pray and sing (16:25). Prayer shook things up again—very literally. The whole earth trembled. Cell doors popped open. Stocks and chains fell from the hands and feet of all the prisoners. Of course it all ended happily. The warden's life was spared because no one escaped, and before the night was over he and his family were Christians.

Does prayer change things? It may not always cause earthquakes, but it will rearrange a lot of situations. The Early Church knew it. Do we?

What a touching scene we see in Acts 20. Paul was saying good-bye for the last time on earth to Christians who were as dear to him as life itself. But what a way to part, even with a breaking heart: "And when he had thus spoken, he kneeled down, and prayed with them all" (20:36).

Farewells are a part of life, but prayer forges a bond that time and distance cannot break. The early Christians never seemed to leave one another's company without committing each other to God in prayer (21:5).

When the crew of the ship bearing Paul to Rome despaired of life after terrible days of a storm, it was a man who had talked to God about the situation who was able to speak words of cheer and comfort (27:21-25).

The Spirit-filled life is inseparably linked with prayer. I hope we have not heard this so much it has lost its meaning. If it has, perhaps we should read and reread Acts until we are impressed anew that unless we pray we are like a soldier on the battlefield without his weapon. Christians in apostolic days didn't do anything until they had prayed. That message is written all over the pages of Acts. God grant that it may get all over us!

5

Salt and Light

The Early Church's Impact on Its Society

Jesus must have startled His followers when He warned that He was sending them out like "sheep in the midst of wolves" (Matthew 10:16). He alerted them to be prepared for actual hatred from the world (John 15:18, 19).

In the New Testament "the world" means society, organized under Satan in opposition to God. The world's philosophy, goals, and life-style are 100-percent antagonistic to God's will and laws. Jesus knew He would build His church in surroundings completely hostile to spirituality, purity, and godliness. The mission of His people is to act as salt and light (Matthew 5:13, 14). In a society that has no taste for spiritual things Christians must bring the salt of the gospel. They are commissioned to take the only light that will dispel humanity's darkness.

We may imagine the Early Church had enviable conditions for its labors. It is true they lived close to the time when Jesus had been on earth. The original group from the Upper Room had seen Him alive after His death. But their world was no more conducive than ours to the kind of living Jesus commanded.

Roman dictatorship held everyone in its iron grip.

The Jews were allowed freedom of worship, but what kind of worship was it? John the Baptist was the first prophetic voice in four centuries. Judaism had its religious hierarchy, and the majority deserved John's epithet "vipers" and Jesus' identification "hypocrites"—playactors.

To the law of Moses a multitude of rules and regulations had been added that no one could really keep. The priests and Pharisees, however, prided themselves on their tedious efforts to do it. There was regular synagogue worship, but it was so encrusted with dead form that it brought no one nearer God. There were a few devout souls like Simeon, Anna, Mary, Joseph, Elisabeth, Zechariah, and others, but they were a tiny minority.

While many have applauded the contributions of Greek culture, its philosophy appealed to the intellect while doing nothing to help anyone find God. It did not stop the rampant spread of idolatry with all of its licentious rites. Great temples had been built to heathen deities, and flagrant immorality was a prominent part of such worship.

Into a Stormy Sea

Into this churning sea of religious decadence, political tyranny, and moral degradation Jesus launched His church. To the natural mind it was a lost cause from the beginning. How could a little group of nobodies survive the pressures they were certain to encounter? It would be only a matter of time until the name of Jesus and the band that called themselves His disciples would be a faded memory. Such reasoning appeared logical to anyone who was ignorant of the Church's supernatural foundation.

Of all places for the Church to begin—Jerusalem!

This was where a violent mob had demanded and accomplished the death of Jesus. But it was also where thousands of Jews had gathered from various parts of the world for the feast days. The Lord saw to it that His church's beginning received maximum exposure.

Events in the Upper Room were soon the hottest topic in the city. The multitude that had gathered around the disciples was stunned. "Confounded" is Luke's word—thrown into confusion, turmoil, and uproar (2:6). The religious crowd was ready to give the newborn Church a hearing. They wanted to know what all of "this" meant. When they heard the explanation, 3,000 of them left the lifeless forms of their old religion and accepted the Christ who had been crucified in that city only a few weeks earlier (2:41).

The gospel is not a thing of cold logic that man can analyze as he would examine some human philosophy. When Christians are full of the Spirit, things will happen that will cause the world to ask, "What meaneth this?" Peter's sermon began with his avowal, "These are not drunken, as ye suppose." Everything the unconverted have ever "supposed" about God and His work has been false and misleading. The Early Church made no effort to cater to the world's reasoning. They boldly proclaimed the truth in plain, everyday language, and the Spirit of God did the rest. It is amazing how many who were first confounded were later converted!

Acts 2:47 makes a surprising observation. At this stage of its short history the Church had "favor with all the people." Jerusalem was becoming a changed city because Christians were faithfully serving their Lord. Opposition would come, but for a time believers enjoyed a favorable climate.

No Ignoring This Crowd!

It did not take long for the hierarchy to get another jolt. It was in the form of a miracle, which we mentioned in a previous chapter (3:1-11). The Sanhedrin's frantic threats show they knew they had something unusual on their hands. The Church was not a pathetic little band carrying on in a small corner and being ignored.

> And they laid hands on them, and put them in hold unto the next day: for it was now eventide. Howbeit many of them which heard the word believed; and the number of the men was about five thousand (4:3, 4).

What a contrast! The apostles were jailed, but many who had heard their message believed and were saved. Let the enemies of Christ do their worst to the preachers. They had turned the Word loose, and there was no prison for it. Isn't that the Church's mission? Turn the Word loose everywhere you can, Christian! Turn it loose in every corner of your community. The Holy Spirit will use the Word like a sharp sword. It will cut through the sins, fears, doubts, and misconceptions of men. Forget the consequences to yourself. Spend, and be spent. Just get the Word out everywhere!

The 10 dozen with which Christ began His church soon became a multitude (4:32). An amazing statement is made in Acts 5:13: "And of the rest durst no man join himself to them: but the people magnified them."

In our day it is the "proper" thing in many circles to have your name on a church roll. It was not that way in those days when the power of God's Spirit surged through His people with such force. People on the outside were awestruck. They were afraid to identify with the believers out of mere curiosity or to be one of the "in" crowd. No one became one of that number just to help his business. Church joining happened only when sinners made a clean break with their sins and committed their lives to Christ without reservation.

It was not long until the church was accused of filling Jerusalem with the message of Jesus (5:28). What a welcome accusation! Wouldn't you like to have your congregation threatened for saturating your town with the gospel?

The tide rolled on. The hand of the Lord reached into the ranks of the religious leadership. Not a few but "a great company" of the Jewish priests left their old traditions for the new life they found in Christ (6:7). The church had now become such a threat to the religious establishment that they resorted to violence and murder to try to stop it. The blood of the first Christian martyr was spilled (7:54-60). But such opposition only fanned the flames. The fire of the Spirit roared on.

Onward and Outward

Samaria was Simon's city. It belonged to him. He ruled the bodies and souls of its people through his sorcery. They considered him "the great power of God" (8:9-11). No one would have dared to attempt to unseat him. But things changed when the message of Jesus came to town. Men and women were freed from the bonds of superstition and the power of the occult. They rejoiced in their freedom in Christ. A whimpering Simon—his little kingdom shattered—could only beseech Peter to pray that God's wrath would not fall on him (8:24).

The gospel reached into "high society" as well as

the ranks of the poor and downtrodden. A prominent official of the Ethiopian government found Christ in the desert through Philip's ministry, as he traveled home without the peace he had gone to Jerusalem to seek (8:26-39).

Our Lord was not content to have a Jewish church while the rest of the world rushed on to eternal damnation. He opened the door to the Gentiles through a Roman army officer (Acts 10). Think of it—Christ had committed disciples in the ranks of Rome's proud legions!

The scattering of Christians from Jerusalem by persecution only enlarged their circle of influence. They used the opportunity to preach Christ in their new localities. Some traveled far, and multitudes came to the Lord (11:19-21). The world became so conscious of the presence of Christ's followers that they finally had to find a name for them (11:26). "Christian" was probably hung on them in derision, but the name stuck. And what could be a better one? May we ever be worthy of it.

Jerusalem was still seething. And things did not get better for those who were determined to stamp out the name of Jesus. When the angel released Peter from prison it created "no small stir" (12:18). The king who had meant to add Peter to his list of victims died a horrible death, "but the word of God grew and multiplied" (12:20-24).

Christ vs. the Occult

The church had a new leader now. He was the former persecutor, Saul, better known to us as Paul. On his first missionary journey with Barnabas, he soon encountered strong occult influence. A sorcerer named Elymas, who had gained a close relationship with a Roman deputy, felt threatened when Paul preached Christ.

As usual, the power of Satan was no match for the Spirit's power. The stunned deputy saw his occultist blinded and left helpless by the stroke of God. Once again the gospel invaded the ranks of government: "Then the deputy, when he saw what was done, believed, being astonished at the doctrine of the Lord" (13:12). He had probably been astonished at some of Elymas' tricks. But what he saw of the Spirit's work made all of that seem like child's play.

Westward the Flame!

Despite fierce opposition from Jewish leaders, Paul's ministry began to reach Gentiles in increasing numbers (13:43-52). Persecution did not keep him and Barnabas from establishing Christian churches along the path of their first journey. The churches began to grow so rapidly that they had to be organized and congregational leaders appointed (14:23).

Now, through Paul, the Holy Spirit sent the message of Christ westward into Europe. Once again direct satanic opposition was encountered and defeated (16:16-18). Silas was Paul's companion now, and they were arrested at Philippi. The conversion of their jailer was another thrilling demonstration of the church's impact on its society.

When God sent the earthquake that jarred the prisoners' bonds loose, the jailer started to commit suicide. When Paul's call stopped him he came crying, "What must I do to be saved?" (16:30). His acceptance of Christ was immediate: "And when he had brought them into his house, he set meat before them, and rejoiced, believing in God with all his

51

house" (16:34). What a change—from a near-suicide to a rejoicing Christian! And all in such a short time.

At Thessalonica the purifying effects of the gospel were so great that Paul and his company were accused of turning the world upside down (17:6). The city government was shaken by the news (v. 8).

We may be inclined to believe our message is for the world's "down and outers" but not for its "upper crust." This is erroneous thinking. We have another example at Beroea that "up and outers" can also be reached for Christ: "Therefore many of them believed; also of honorable women which were Greeks, and of men, not a few" (17:12).

Paul spent a little time in Athens. Although his stay was short and the results do not seem spectacular, there were followers of Christ there when the apostle left: "Howbeit certain men clave unto him, and believed: among the which was Dionysius the Areopagite, and a woman named Damaris, and others with them" (17:34).

Churches in Unlikely Places

Corinth was such a wicked city that the word *Corinthian* is still in our dictionary. "A gay profligate man" is one of Mr. Webster's definitions. This is putting it mildly. Anyone looking at Corinth would have said it was the last place there would ever be a thriving church. But the power of the Spirit swept into that satanic stronghold as Paul and his company went there to preach.

It was not a short visit. Paul stayed a year and a half (18:11). He must have been disturbed over the entrenched evil, for the Lord appeared to him in a vision at night to reassure him. "I have much people in this city," God said. Amazing! Much people in

Corinth? Yes. They were still in the tight clutches of the devil, but that would be changed. The liberating force of the Spirit of God was about to snap the chains that bound multitudes in wild, dissolute Corinth.

Despite widespread Jewish opposition, many dispersed Jews accepted Jesus as their Messiah and Saviour. The eloquent Apollos was used in a tremendous ministry to them: "For he mightily convinced the Jews, and that publicly, showing by the Scriptures that Jesus was Christ" (18:28).

Paul established a church in Ephesus whose outreach was so great the Bible says concerning it: "And this continued [Paul's ministry] by the space of two years; so that all they which dwelt in Asia [Asia Minor] heard the word of the Lord Jesus, both Jews and Greeks" (19:10).

Ephesus was another occult stronghold. But the salt and light of the Church were at work. There was a public burning of books of "curious arts" by people who had been delivered from this satanic bondage (19:19).

Christian influence at Ephesus became so widespread that the men who earned their living making silver shrines for the heathen goddess Diana instigated a near riot. Their complaint was a tribute to the gospel's power. They shouted that in almost all of Asia Minor there was danger of men forsaking the worship of Diana (19:26, 27). These silversmiths saw real danger to their livelihood because the number of Christians was growing so rapidly.

When Paul became a prisoner his ministry was not stifled. It was only turned in different directions. His message of Christ made the Roman governor Felix tremble (24:25). Paul was the man on whom the crew of the prison ship leaned for moral support during the storm that finally destroyed their vessel (27:21-

36). The shipwreck that landed them on the island of Melita was the means of carrying the message of Jesus there through the miracles the people saw (28:1-10). Even in Rome under house arrest, Paul spread the light in the empire's capital city by his untiring testimony to the Lord Jesus (28:30, 31).

The society of those days knew there was a Church. It felt the mighty authority of the name the Church proclaimed—Jesus.

6

Growing Pains

The Early Church's Internal Problems

The more the Church is under attack by the world, the less severe its internal problems are likely to be. Persecution has a way of driving people together. Trouble from the outside tends to minimize difficulties on the inside.

Nevertheless, problems are the price of growth, and the Early Church was not immune to dissension in its ranks. Christians are people, and even saved people can experience difficulties in their relationships with each other.

The multiplication of problems accompanying expansion is one reason the church must be organized. The apostle Paul, in his Spirit-imparted wisdom, was careful to appoint leaders and establish a measure of organization in the churches that sprang up under his ministry. Without recognized authority in the church, differences that should be solved quickly may produce chaos.

Throughout the first four chapters of Acts, no problems are recorded within the church. There was too much excitement over its explosive growth. Days and nights vibrated with revival. Who would spoil the beauty of such an atmosphere? But someone did.

The spirit of brotherhood in those early days prompted the Christians to share their earthly goods. At the close of Acts 4 Luke mentions that Barnabas brought the money from the sale of his property and turned it over to the apostles. However, we notice that chapter 5 starts with "But." A discordant note was about to jar the tranquility of God's people.

Lies in Church

Ananias and his wife Sapphira were members of the Early Church, but they were not around for long. After the church established a fund to help the poor, this couple attempted to deceive the apostles by lying about their contributions. Judgment was swift in their case.

Verse 2 indicates that Ananias was the instigator of their scheme, but Sapphira was "privy to it." Apparently she did nothing to influence her husband to abandon his fatal course. "Sapphira" means "Beautiful." How tragic that she did not live up to her name. She was like some people since that day who have an outward profession but are ugly and carnal inside.

Peter's admonition to Ananias does not sound like the apostles had required the believers to give all their money to the church. Some (like Barnabas) did so, but it seems to have been of their own free will. The sin of Ananias and Sapphira was in their pretense. Obviously they craved recognition without sacrifice.

If Satan cannot destroy the Church he will try to discredit it. One of his most successful means of hindering the Lord's work is to create discord and division. The church's unity is always under bombardment from the devil's heavy guns. The spirit of the Christians had been like a solid wall. Ananias and Sapphira made the first crack. It was a small one, but that is the way big cracks start.

How disastrous that this couple had lost their spiritual sensitivity. Apparently they did not consider that the Lord of the Church would reveal their sin to its leadership. Peter did not have ESP. He was full of the Holy Spirit, and the Spirit quickly flashed the information to him when Ananias gave him the money. The indictment was one you would not expect to hear in such company: "Why hath Satan filled thine heart to lie to the Holy Ghost?" (5:3).

The Greek word used here for "filled" means "to make replete; to cram." The shocker is that this happened to people associated with a thriving Pentecostal church! Such a condition doesn't happen overnight. It is no spur-of-the-moment occurrence. It creeps up slowly—just as a container is filled ever so gradually but surely with water oozing into it. Satan doesn't sweep into a Christian's heart; he seeps in. The way to avoid such a catastrophe is to keep Satan completely out of your heart. Allow him no space at all.

Cooperating With Satan

Let's shift gears for a moment. Peter declared that Satan had filled Ananias' heart, but in verse 4 he asked, "Why hast *thou* conceived this thing?" No matter how much the devil tries to influence an individual, that person must make the final decision to sin. No one can truthfully say, "The devil made me do it." Satan may suggest it very strongly, but you have to do it.

The Greek word for "conceived" in verse 4 indicates a deliberate purpose. This answers Peter's question in verse 3—"Why hath Satan filled thine heart?" It was because Ananias himself had first embraced the idea. Satan had to have his cooperation.

The fact that a person could deteriorate spiritually to such a low point in the midst of powerful movings of the Spirit shows the human responsibility that always exists in the spiritual realm. Being in a heavenly atmosphere does not automatically ensure we will remain in a high spiritual state. We are not robots. We are free moral agents, and even the Spirit of God will not violate our power of choice.

When Sapphira came, unmindful of her husband's sudden death, she confirmed the lie he had told. Again Peter's accusation was swift: "How is it that ye have agreed together to tempt the Spirit of the Lord?" (5:9). To tempt God is to see how far you can go before He intervenes. It is dangerous business. To that the fresh graves of Ananias and Sapphira bore strong witness.

The severity of God's judgment on this couple shows how much He abhors religious make-believe. Jesus' strongest words of denunciation were reserved for hypocrites. Ananias and Sapphira pretended a complete consecration to God, but their dedication was partial—or even lacking.

Imagine the shock if such games of deceit in church still resulted in death. What if every Christian who falsely declares, "I've had a bad year and really have nothing on which to pay tithes," were struck dead? The pastor would have to get help preaching funerals. Usually in this age of grace God does not move in such fashion. We may wonder why He does not intervene drastically when we see problems that seem to demand it.

But think what it would mean if He always did. People would carry out God's commands because of terror, not love. The church would be full of robots who make each move because they think it is one that will avoid divine wrath. There would be constant tension instead of the joyous liberty of the Spirit.

In this case the church was young. God in His wisdom saw that if such playacting went unchecked it could become a cancer in the body of Christ. Acts 5 starts off like a chapter from the Old Testament, but thank God for His swift action. Some may feel that nothing but a "Smile, God loves you" atmosphere should prevail in the church. The positive accent, is good, but it is proper for a wholesome fear to settle down over us from time to time. Too much of the light, shallow, and frothy without the fear of the Lord is destructive to spirituality.

Murmuring Christians

The next internal problem in the church had a completely different origin. It was simply the result of so many people coming in so fast. Growing pains are a pleasant form of suffering, but they can produce frustration that has to be dealt with.

Did you think there was never any "murmuring" in a congregation of Spirit-filled people? Read Acts 6:1. What produced the undercurrent of complaining? "And in those days, when the number of the disciples was multiplied"—growth, expansion, progress. Multitudes of people were congregating together, and they rubbed each other the wrong way at times.

The "Grecians" were Jews from outside Palestine who spoke Greek. The "Hebrews" were mostly

Palestinian Jews who spoke Aramaic. Whether the complaint was justified we do not know. Undoubtedly the Grecians felt like outsiders. They were away from home. Who can blame them if they had grown a little edgy? When food was apportioned among the church's widows the Grecians noticed anything that looked like discrimination. They were Christians, but they were also humans—just like us. When you have humans on the scene, the potential for problems is always present.

The apostles were wise men, and they needed wisdom to handle this touchy situation. Here was an emotional issue that could have fragmented the young church. Blundering hands could have produced an eventual explosion.

The task of food distribution was getting bigger every day. It might be assumed from the context that the apostles had been taking most of the responsibility. But they saw what would happen if they continued. It was all a worthy and necessary work, but there was another work that must take precedence for these men. Their chief responsibility was to provide spiritual leadership. The ministry of the Word would be effective only if they gave themselves continually to prayer. If they allowed themselves to be sidetracked, priority number one would be replaced by priority number two.

From Murmuring to Pleasure

The principle that emerged from the solution of this problem has not changed. Ministers today are not usually confronted with the daily task of feeding a large crowd. But in our complex society a multitude of interests can claim a leader's time and strength and leave nothing for his spiritual ministry. Who suffers because of this? The whole church.

"It is not reason that we should leave the word of God, and serve tables" (6:2). Thank God for that manifesto. The tables must be served, but a division of responsibility had to be made. How beautifully the Spirit flowed through the body of believers as this sensitive issue was resolved. The apostles did not abdicate their God-ordained leadership. They were the ones through whom the Spirit provided the solution. Their decision to find seven qualified men "pleased the whole multitude." What a change—from murmuring to pleasure!

Note how carefully the apostles set forth the qualifications of the seven. This was not a popularity contest. No one was to be chosen for his magnetic personality, prestige, wealth, or ability to make pleasing conversation. There were three simple but plain requirements. The seven men must be (1) of honest report, (2) full of the Holy Spirit, and (3) full of wisdom. When you can find men like that to take the administrative load off a pastor's shoulders, there is no limit to the church's potential.

The procedure protected both the authority of the apostles and the rights of the congregation. The people chose the seven. But these men did not assume their task until they had been brought before the apostles, who prayerfully laid their hands on them to ordain them to their offices.

What was the result? The flow of revival, which may have been temporarily slowed by the tension in the church, burst out again. "And the word of God increased; and the number of the disciples multiplied in Jerusalem greatly; and a great company of the priests were obedient to the faith" (6:7).

Certain Men

The next serious problem that overtook the church was doctrinal: "And certain men which came down from Judea taught the brethren, and said, Except ye be circumcised after the manner of Moses, ye cannot be saved" (15:1).

The church has frequently been plagued by "certain men coming down and teaching" things that divide and disturb. Like those described in this verse, they invariably sway many by their dogmatism. They are right; everyone else is wrong. Who was it that these agitators taught? "The brethren,"—where it would do the most damage.

Such activity brought depression and bondage. The teachers were "troubling . . . with words" and "subverting [the] souls" of their listeners (15:24). Paul and Barnabas soon encountered these "certain men" and had "no small dissension and disputation with them" (v. 2).

This Judaistic teaching had support among Pharisees who had accepted Christ (v. 5). It is not unknown for people to carry erroneous teaching from the past over into their Christian lives for a time. But problems can develop if they continue to embrace error and insist it is truth.

This issue could not be resolved simply by letting it smolder and hoping it would finally die. It is a relief to read in verse 6: "And the apostles and elders came together for to consider of this matter." When Christians who disagree can come together to reason, the chasm that separates them has a way of shrinking. It is when they refuse to talk that positions harden and animosities develop.

Things were tense when the meeting began, but they may not have been quite as hot as the King James Version sounds. Verse 7 speaks of "much disputing." The *New American Standard Bible* says "much debate." Here were men with strong and opposing convictions. They are to be congratulated for thoroughly airing their problem. Everyone spoke his mind freely—this was good. It is when we bottle up our feelings and let them fester that we are headed for trouble.

There was a lull in the discussion, and Peter stood up (v. 7). His testimony carried weight, for there had been no more devoted observer of Jewish customs. As Peter related how God had used him to take the gospel to the Gentiles, the extreme Judaizers in the group began to soften. This paved the way for Paul and Barnabas to speak at length on their ministry to the Gentiles. The Spirit of God was quieting hearts, for the highly charged meeting had settled down into silence (v. 12). Strong-minded men were holding their peace (v. 13).

The Word of Wisdom

Clearly James was motivated by the Spirit in enunciating the obvious consensus of the group after their "much debate." His decision had a firm scriptural basis. What God was doing agreed with Old Testament prophecies. He was saving people outside Israel. The troubling of the Gentile Christians must stop. Since there were certain practices that offended the Jews, the church's leaders would ask the Gentiles to avoid them. That was all.

Letters to the Gentile churches were drafted, announcing the decision of the apostles and elders. What better messengers could be found to deliver them than Paul and Barnabas? Two others, Judas Barsabas and Silas, completed the party.

The decision reached by the council is a balanced

picture of what the Christian life should be. The gospel is not a burden: "For it seemed good to the Holy Ghost, and to us, to lay upon you no greater burden than these necessary things" (15:28). On the other hand, our salvation does not free us of all responsibility to others. There are some "necessary things" to which we must carefully attend. Abstaining from fornication is something Christians should do without being told, for it is an outright sin. The other things mentioned (v. 29) were offensive to so many people that the testimony of the Gentile Christians would be damaged if they engaged in them.

Those men found the mind of the Spirit. What seemed good to Him became good to them (v. 28). The Church moved on. There would be other problems, but the Holy Spirit and earnest believers would solve them together.

7

Things They Most Surely Believed

The Early Church's Theology

Don't expect to find a fully developed system of theology in Acts. That is not the purpose of the Book. It is Church history. The Holy Spirit gave us the whole New Testament because one book cannot contain all the facets of our many-splendored gospel.

Acts supplies the action. The Epistles, especially Paul's, unfold the doctrines in more detail. When you read Acts you seem to be running down the road in a cloud of dust, trying to keep up with the fast-paced events. In Romans you feel you are in the classroom of a great theologian.

Spiritual experience and activity cannot be divorced from theology. Belief in certain teachings was important to the Early Church. Luke, the author of Acts, had already written his gospel "to set forth in order a declaration of those things which are most surely believed among us" (Luke 1:1).

Anyone who implies it makes no difference what you believe as long as you have certain experiences finds no support in Acts. The beliefs of the Early Church were simple, but definite and strong. Its members stayed with the basics. Perhaps theology has sometimes tried to spread itself too thin and lost some of its vitality.

A brief reference to or an omission of some truth in Acts should not be interpreted as a sign it was not believed. Luke was writing one book, not volumes. In the remainder of this chapter we will look at some of the truths that formed the Early Church's foundation of faith.

God the Father

The Early Church believed in a God who was very personal. To them He was not earth's absentee landlord. They called Him "Father" (2:33). They believed He was calling people to himself so they might be saved (2:39). He was the object of their unceasing worship and adoration (2:47). He was the God of history—the God of Abraham, Isaac, and Jacob (3:13), who guided and ruled the affairs of men (4:28).

In a world where the heathen had all kinds of explanations for the existence of the universe, the early Christians believed God was its Creator (4:24). Paul boldly took this belief to Athens, the famous center of culture and learning (17:22-29). In the same sermon he declared that this all-powerful Creator would reveal himself to earnest seekers, to whom He is always close (v. 27).

Jesus Christ, the Center of Everything

No true member of the Apostolic Church considered Jesus a mere man or a teacher who simply happened to be ahead of His time. The chief cornerstone of the church's belief was that Jesus is the incarnate Son of God. He was their divine Center around which all other truths revolved. That company did not teach that Jesus was one of many ways to God. Peter could not have put it more forcefully than his testimony to the Jewish religious leaders: "Neither is there salvation in any other: for there is none other name under heaven given among men, whereby we must be saved" (4:12).

Jesus' resurrection from the dead was the Early Church's great theme. Had He died and remained in the grave He would have been only a wonderful memory. But His resurrection confirmed He was all He claimed to be. That message became a trumpet blast, piercing the atmosphere of pagan idolatry and lifeless Judaism.

Peter cried to his startled audience at Pentecost that it was Jesus "whom God hath raised up, having loosed the pains of death: because it was not possible that he should be holden of it" (2:24). He exulted over His ascension: "Therefore being by the right hand of God exalted, and having received of the Father the promise of the Holy Ghost, he hath shed forth this, which ye now see and hear" (2:33). That is a doctrinal statement if there ever was one!

Peter kept preaching: "Therefore let all the house of Israel know assuredly, that God hath made that same Jesus, whom ye have crucified, both Lord and Christ" (2:36). Hear it! Jesus is Lord; the Father's Anointed One. Only because Jesus is God did Peter dare tell a cripple to rise and walk in His name (3:6). No one could be rightly called "the Prince of life" if he were only a man—even a good man (3:15).

The Early Church believed Jesus would return to earth. You can be sure no one forgot the angels' promise of this (1:11). After the healing of the lame man Peter urged the crowd:

Repent ye therefore, and be converted, that your sins

may be blotted out, when the times of refreshing shall come from the presence of the Lord; and he shall send Jesus Christ, which before was preached unto you: whom the heaven must receive until the times of restitution of all things, which God hath spoken by the mouth of all his holy prophets since the world began" (3:19-21).

Paul enunciated the church's strong conviction that Jesus redeems sinners, not by His teaching or moral example, but by His shed blood (20:28: ". . . the church of God, which he hath purchased with his own blood").

The Holy Spirit

That the early Christians believed in the Holy Spirit as a Person there can be no doubt. On the Day of Pentecost they quickly recognized a divine personality had filled them. Furthermore, Peter assured the multitude that the Spirit would make His home in all who accept Jesus Christ as Lord and Saviour (2:38, 39).

Who could lie to a nebulous, indefinable influence? You can lie only to a person, and Peter accused Ananias and Sapphira of lying to the Holy Spirit. They tested His forbearance to see how far they could go before He stopped them (5:3, 9).

The first martyr, Stephen, accused his tormentors of resisting the Holy Spirit (7:51). Such a statement is reasonable only if he was speaking of a person.

Being full of the Holy Spirit was a fundamental requirement for leadership in the church (6:3).

Paul was concerned when he found professed disciples who obviously lacked the Spirit's presence in their lives (19:1-6). The apostles were anxious that all Christians be filled with the Spirit without delay (8:14-17). The Spirit of God was not ignored by the members of the Early Church. He was not the unknown member of the Trinity to them. A vital part of Paul's first experience with Christ was his infilling with the Spirit (9:17). When God opened the door of mercy to the Gentiles, their salvation and baptism in the Spirit were virtually simultaneous (10:44).

Peter received a personal message of guidance from the Spirit (11:12). The first great missionary effort of the Church was launched because the congregation at Antioch was given a specific directive from the Spirit, naming the very men they should send (13:2, 4). When a vital doctrinal question arose, the church's leaders could not be comfortable until they were sure they had the mind of the Spirit (15:28).

The Inspiration of the Scriptures

The authority with which the first disciples preached stunned every audience. They had a strong conviction that every word of Scripture came directly from God. Can anyone doubt this was what produced such authoritative preaching? When they quoted passages from the Old Testament they declared that these were the words of the Holy Spirit (1:16). At Pentecost Peter assured the people they were seeing the fulfillment of prophecy (2:17, 25-31). The confidence of those early preachers in the Scriptures as the sure foundation of their message is plain to see (3:22-25; 4:11). They were certain that when those men wrote the Scriptures God was speaking through them (4:25, 26). Stephen's whole defense was based on the Scriptures (Acts 7).

James' word of wisdom at the conclusion of the meeting in Acts 15 was linked to Scripture (vv. 15-17). Paul's ministry consisted largely of reasoning from the Scriptures (17:2). Apollos was "mighty in the Scriptures" (18:24). His ministry to the Jews was highly effective because he used the Scriptures to prove Jesus is Christ (18:28).

Future Judgment

While the church proclaimed salvation through Christ, it also warned of judgment on those who reject Him. Paul did not mute this unpleasant truth even when he was among the intellectuals (17:30, 31). Peter quoted Moses' warning about the sure destruction of those who turn away from Christ (3:23). Paul sounded a similar warning to the people at Antioch in Pisidia (13:41). When his message was rejected, he and Barnabas told them they had cut themselves off from everlasting life by their own actions (13:46). This could only mean their fate would be everlasting death. Felix trembled when Paul reasoned of "righteousness, temperance, and judgment to come" (24:25).

The Church

Paul received the revelation of the mystery of the Church. This mystery is that Jew and Gentile have been brought together in one body in Christ. But even at Cornelius' house Peter began to sense this. When he was confronted by other leaders he demonstrated that this unfolding truth had not lost its grip on him. Being spiritually sensitive men, the others accepted the concept of the Church as a body of all believers (11:1-18).

Not all of the church offices Paul names in his epistles are enumerated in Acts, but we see some of their functions. The word *deacon* is not used of the seven who took over the task of feeding the widows, but they were surely functioning as deacons. The word *elders* appears frequently in Acts. There was leadership ordained by God, and those Spirit-filled people recognized and accepted it.

The very word *church* ("a calling out") indicates Christians are expected to be separated from the life-style of the ungodly. Peter implored his audience at Pentecost not only to accept Christ but also to keep themselves from the sins of their age (2:40). A life of holiness, sanctification, and separation was expected of everyone who named the name of Christ. Any other kind of living was unthinkable for a member of the Church.

Two ordinances were observed constantly. Water baptism was not an option converts could choose if they felt so inclined. It was a part of Christ's command (Matthew 28:19) and was strictly adhered to by the Early Church (2:38). The "breaking [of] bread" (2:46) was undoubtedly the observance of the Lord's Supper. This was a regular part of church meetings (Acts 20:7). In those days it involved a whole meal and was a time of wonderful fellowship.

Prayer for the sick was always a part of the church's life (5:15, 16). More will be said about this ministry of healing in the next chapter.

Angels

We must not rely on artists for our concept of angels. They often draw on their imagination or folklore instead of Scripture. Some pictures almost convey the impression that angels and fairies (and other imaginary creatures) are in the same category. Not so.

The early Christians believed in angels and were often the beneficiaries of their ministry. They accepted the message two angels brought them immediately after Jesus' ascension (1:10, 11). Some of the disciples were delivered from prison by angels (5:19; 12:7). Philip received guidance from the angel of the Lord about the direction of his evangelistic travels (8:26). An angel instructed Cornelius to send for Peter so he could hear the gospel (10:3-7). The angel of the Lord struck Herod with a fatal disease (12:23). And the angel of God visited Paul to reassure him during a raging storm at sea (27:23).

Satan

The early Christians did not consider Satan a myth like Santa Claus. Nor did they believe he is an impersonal influence of some kind. They knew he is an evil personality who was their constant foe. Because they belonged to Christ and were filled with His Spirit, they did not cringe in fear before Satan, but neither did they take him lightly.

Peter recognized Satan was behind the attempted deception by two church members (5:3). Such an infiltration of the church's ranks is indicative of the devil's tireless attacks on the work of God.

Paul's divine commission was to turn people "from the power of Satan unto God" (26:18). The apostle called a sorcerer the devil's child (13:10). Peter declared that during Jesus' earthly ministry He healed people whom Satan had oppressed (10:38).

Demons

The word *demon* is not in the King James Version. "Devils, evil spirits, unclean spirits"—these are some of the words it uses. "Demons" is the translation in most other versions.

Although no one in the Early Church wrote a book

on demonology, the Christians were well aware of the existence and work of demons. Part of Jesus' charge to them was to deliver people from demonic power. (See Mark 16:17.) Clearly they carried out this commission (5:16; 8:7; 16:16-18; 19:11, 12). It should be said, however, that their awareness of demons did not cause them to be preoccupied with the subject.

Excuse the Brevity

Volumes have been written on these subjects. I have had to compress my comments into one chapter, and I have not quoted every Scripture passage on every doctrine. I hope I have not become tedious by quoting too many. Anything but a quick look at these truths is impossible in a few pages, and is beyond the purpose of this book. Textbooks on theology deal with additional doctrines which I do not have the space to mention. Those to which I have called your attention are what seem to me to be the most vital.

We do not see the Church in Acts trying to compose formal creeds. We simply observe Christians with flaming hearts on the move with the message of the crucified and risen Christ. It remained for others to crystallize many of the Church's teachings and give us a sharper view of them. Paul was the one the Holy Spirit used most in the theological field in the Apostolic Church.

The Church did not have a fully prepared statement of faith the day after Pentecost. But the beliefs were there, and in due time God used His servants to bring them into clearer focus. This was to help Christians of all times understand the certainty of the things they most surely believe.

8

Signs That Followed

Miracles in the Early Church

One conspicuous aspect of Jesus' ministry was His miracles. Each time a miracle occurred in the Early Church it was a reminder that Jesus is alive.

Our Lord's greatest miracle was His resurrection from the dead—the raising up in 3 days of the temple His enemies thought they had destroyed (John 2:19-21). Believe this miracle, and there is no problem accepting all the others.

The Miracle of Pentecost

Not all miracles are physical healings. Pentecost was a miracle. It was a sign to doubters and unbelievers that Jesus is ascended and reigning. The Jews from various parts of the world who heard the Christians praising God in their own languages knew they had encountered something extraordinary. Peter declared that the outpouring of the Spirit, with its accompanying sign of tongues, was an open declaration that Jesus is at His Father's right hand (2:33).

The Healing of the Lame Man

God specializes in confounding the wisdom of

men who imagine they can find a natural explanation for everything. The first miracle of healing recorded in Acts is an example (3:1-10). The object of divine mercy on that occasion was a man who had never taken a step in his life. Either because of a birth defect or an accident at birth, he was doomed to spend his life as a cripple.

Can you imagine the times during his boyhood that he longed to run and play as he saw others doing? But this was not to be his lot. Everyone who knew him assumed he would live and die with his handicap.

This man was fortunate to have kind friends who came to his home every day and carried him to the temple gate. There he could receive at least a small amount of money as alms. This was as much as anyone could do for him. Those who loved him most could not give him the power to walk. Neither could Peter and John—but they were well acquainted with Someone who could.

Peter was quite truthful when he admitted he had no silver or gold to give the man. But what he had was far more valuable. "Such as I have give I thee." Christian, do you realize what you have? If you do, are you giving it?

Everything seemed to happen almost simultaneously. As Peter commanded the lame man to ruse up and walk in the name of Jesus, he reached down and grasped his hand. There was no gradual flow of life to the shriveled limbs. It happened "immediately." The record says his feet and ankle bones received strength. He did not need the help of Peter's outstretched hand. "He leaping up stood, and walked"

(3:8). As he got inside the temple grounds he did what anyone else would have done. He began to leap again, praising God in what surely must have been a loud voice.

The reaction of the crowd was predictable. "All the people ran together" (3:11). No one doubted something extraordinary had happened. What they wanted to know was, "How?"

Peter lost no time answering them. First came his stinging accusations for their part in Jesus' death. They were tempered by his statement that he recognized they had done it in ignorance (3:17). The healing, he declared, revealed the power of the crucified One who was no longer dead: "And his name, through faith in his name, hath made this man strong" (3:16).

Physical miracles often illustrate the greater spiritual miracles of the gospel. It is astounding for a cripple to walk. But it is even more miraculous when a spiritual cripple receives strength to abandon his old life and start walking in the way of righteousness. The lame man at the gate was no more helpless than people who are bound by sin and cannot lift themselves out of their condition. Deliverance comes to them only through the name of Jesus. Every man is born into the world a spiritual cripple, and he will never walk until the power of the risen Christ fills his life.

A Spiritual Explosion

This miracle was a bombshell in Jerusalem. The religious leaders thought they had put the "Jesus religion" out of business. Now the news was spreading throughout the city that one of its best known beggars was walking for the first time and giving Jesus the praise for it!

Can you help smiling as you read of their quandary? They were "grieved" over this kind of activity (4:2). The temple guard was sent, and Peter and John were whisked away to spend the night in custody. Peter was never bolder. Yes, he testified, it was by the name of Jesus this man had been made whole. Jesus is the world's only Saviour and He has risen from the dead (4:8-11).

It is hard to argue against results. The lame man had been arrested with the apostles and was standing—not lying—in front of them (4:10). Listen to this: "And beholding the man which was healed standing with them, they could say nothing against it" (4:14). The religious hierarchy was in the midst of a hurricane. Five thousand new converts were swept into the church after this miracle (v. 4). The most the priests could do was threaten the apostles, but their words fell on deaf ears.

What a scene when those men got back to church! As soon as they were released they went where Christians always go—"to their own company." The praises of the congregation swelled like one mighty voice. They asked the Lord for more boldness and more miracles, and God responded. The meeting place shook with His power and everyone received a fresh filling of the Spirit (4:31). They witnessed to Christ with more courage than ever, and the hurricane swept on.

Too Many to Record

Luke did not have the space in Acts to record all the miracles of those days, anymore than John did in his Gospel (John 20:30; 21:25). But it is plain that signs followed the church's ministry continually:

> And by the hands of the apostles were many signs and wonders wrought among the people. . . . They brought forth the sick into the streets. . . . There came also a multitude . . . , bringing sick folks, and them which were vexed with unclean spirits: and they were healed every one (5:12, 15, 16).

The purpose of these signs is brought into focus in verse 14: "And believers were the more added to the Lord, multitudes both of men and women." God does not display His power to dazzle, but to convert.

The ministry of Stephen was accompanied by "great wonders and miracles" (6:8). The Samaritan revival under Philip's leadership was the scene of many healings and deliverances from demons (8:6, 7, 13). Stephen and Philip were not apostles, they were what would be called laymen today.

The Raising of Dorcas

What a radiant character was this lady from the seaport city of Joppa. Her Aramaic name was Tabitha. In Greek it was Dorcas, meaning gazelle. It was an appropriate name for one whose life was so full of beauty and grace.

If Dorcas were living today she might be known as a deaconess. Her ministry was serving others. "Full of good works and almsdeeds" is the Bible's description of her (9:36). Some churches still call their women's group the Dorcas Society.

Dorcas had a special work among the church's widows. Without any means of supporting themselves, who knows how many would have been in rags if it had not been for her devoted hands. How untiringly and joyfully she labored to make their clothing (9:39).

Can you imagine the blow to the Joppa church when Dorcas died? Lovingly the Christians did all they could. In preparation for her burial they washed her body and laid her in the privacy of an upstairs room (9:37).

Did that congregation expect a miracle, or did they call for Peter only for the comfort he could bring them? I suspect at least a few of them believed death had not had the last word.

When Peter arrived he found the expected scene of sadness. Being a Christian does not keep one from grieving for those he has lost in death. Can you doubt that Peter wiped tears from his own eyes as he entered the room? The widows brought the clothes Dorcas had made for them. What a tribute to a life that was spent solely for others! As the bereaved women moved about the room saying, "Look at what she made for me," their tears flowed unashamedly.

But the scene of death and grief was soon to be changed. Peter sensed what God wanted him to do. Why did he order everyone out of the room? I do not believe it was done in harshness. But it is not easy to exercise faith when you are surrounded by people who are full of sorrow.

There was such simplicity in Peter's actions. A few simple words describe what surely seems the greatest of all miracles—the raising of the dead. The apostle "kneeled down, and prayed; and turning him to the body said, Tabitha, arise. And she opened her eyes: and when she saw Peter, she sat up" (9:40). Of course he quickly led her out to the tearful company. What a camp meeting there must have been for the next few hours! But did God raise Dorcas only to alleviate sorrow? No. Verse 42 tells us the purpose of the miracle: "And it was known throughout all Joppa; and *many believed in the Lord.*"

The Healing of the Cripple at Lystra

A miracle nearly identical to the first one recorded in Acts happened at Lystra under Paul's ministry. Again there was a man who had been born a cripple and had never walked. Paul did not encounter him on his way to the temple as Peter and John had the beggar in Acts 3. This time Paul was preaching, and the man was in his congregation: "The same heard Paul speak"—faith was generated in his heart through the Word (14:9). To Paul the Holy Spirit flashed the perception that this faith was present. Without hesitation the apostle shouted, "Stand upright on thy feet." There is no indication Paul even touched him. In an instant the man "leaped and walked" (v. 10).

The audience was Gentile, not Jewish. The people quickly acknowledged the miracle, but attributed it to Paul and Barnabas being gods (v. 11). Spirit-filled men cannot enjoy undue adulation. Paul could have basked in the glow of the crowd's slavish worship, but he would not permit such a thing for a moment. He and Barnabas had to almost fight off the mob physically. Frantically, Paul explained it was God's power, not his, that had raised up the lame man.

The outcome of this miracle was different. We do not read of a great revival breaking out. Jewish agitators soon arrived and "persuaded the people" (14:19). The fickleness of human nature is displayed by the change in these people. The same crowd that had been ready to worship Paul now helped stone him. Thinking he was dead, they callously dragged him out of the city and left what they assumed was his lifeless body lying in its own blood. But with what was obviously supernatural strength, Paul arose and went to Derbe (14:20).

Perhaps this account is in the Bible to help us avoid discouragement if we do not always see great multitudes brought to Christ after they witness miracles. Men are free moral agents, and sin is a great hardener of hearts. Some people are so enslaved by Satan that they could see the dead raised in front of their eyes and still turn away from Christ.

Even though the record is silent about the number of converts at Lystra, there must have been some. God's Word never returns to Him void. Could you doubt for a moment that the man who was healed remained a disciple of Jesus? We will not know until eternity, but we must remember our responsibility is to be faithful in our witnessing and leave the results with God.

Miracles in the Heart of Heathendom

Paul's ministry at Ephesus was marked by "special miracles" (19:11). When the sick could not be brought to him, "from his body were brought unto the sick handkerchiefs or aprons, and the diseases departed from them, and the evil spirits went out of them" (v. 12). Note the difference shown in this passage between physical disease and demon possession. Demons may cause sickness, but not all sickness can be attributed to them. We must be careful not to identify every disease with a demon.

Paul's miracle-packed ministry had a powerful effect on the heathen stronghold of Ephesus and the surrounding territory. The Word reached much of Asia Minor (19:10). People who had been enslaved by Satan through occult practices publicly renounced their old way of life by burning their books of "curious arts" (v. 19).

Even when Paul was on his way to Rome as a prisoner the Lord confirmed his ministry with miracles. When he and the other passengers from the wrecked ship landed at Melita (now Malta) the natives showed them great kindness. As Paul gathered sticks to help start a fire he apparently did not notice a sleeping snake curled up in the branches. When it was awakened by the heat it bit Paul. The superstitious onlookers decided he must be a fugitive and was being punished for his crimes. After he suffered no ill effects from the bite, they concluded he was a god (28:1-6).

Jesus spoke of His disciples taking up serpents (Mark 16:18). This miracle is an example of what He meant. Paul was not deliberately handling snakes to show off his power. The whole incident was a misfortune that befell him while he was about his business for Christ, and the Lord intervened.

Before Paul left Malta he laid his hands on the sick island chief and prayed the prayer of faith. Following this, many people came for healing (28:8, 9). Luke does not tell us how many accepted Christ as Saviour as a result of this ministry. We can be sure, however, that a strong testimony to Christ was left on Malta. The miracles got the attention of the people as nothing else would have.

"The Lord working with them." That is the story that began in an upper room.

9

Channels of Power

Spiritual Gifts in the Early Church

The gifts of the Spirit are His supernatural operations through individuals to meet needs that arise in the course of the Church's ministry.

Paul explained that Spirit-filled Christians have "gifts differing according to the grace that is given to us" (Romans 12:6). This verse emphasizes two important principles: First, the gifts of the Spirit are by grace, which forbids our boasting over them. Second, by God's own wise design, they differ. This makes it unreasonable for anyone to despair if the gifts manifested through him do not seem as important as those of others.

Jesus did not describe to His disciples the gifts that would function through them after Pentecost. They were not ready for such teaching. As the Church ministered under the Spirit's anointing these manifestations appeared and were recognized as His gifts.

To Paul, the Holy Spirit gave the assignment of providing our New Testament teaching about spiritual gifts. By the time he wrote to the Corinthians some guidelines were necessary. We look to 1 Corinthians 12 through 14 for Paul's main exposition. There is also a list of spiritual gifts in Romans 12:6-8. You will notice some overlapping in these passages, but each one adds something. When they are put together we have a composite list of spiritual gifts.

Since Paul's readers understood the nature of the gifts, he did not stop after naming each one and describe its exercise. Where, then, do we get our enlightenment? Early Church history is recorded in Acts, so isn't it logical to look there? We find no passage in Acts expounding the gifts, but it seems reasonable to expect to discover ministries there which we now recognize as gifts of the Holy Spirit.

The gifts named in 1 Corinthians 12:8-10 fall rather naturally into three areas: revelation, power, and utterance. We will consider them in that order.

Gifts of Revelation

These gifts bring revelations by the Spirit that are obtainable in no other way. The word of wisdom involves the application of that information, often in the form of counsel. It is conceivable the word of wisdom and the word of knowledge may sometimes be joined together.

The word of wisdom was undoubtedly manifested through the apostles' spokesman (probably Peter) in Acts 6:2-4. A serious problem threatened the church's unity, but the matter was resolved when the Spirit gave His judgment through its leadership.

We have a clear example of the word of wisdom in Acts 15:13-21. After a long debate, James delivered his decision, which expressed the mind of the Holy Spirit. It had a strong scriptural content, using Old Testament prophecy as a foundation. It was not something the apostle had reasoned out. Through the inspiration of the Spirit he saw the answer to the dilemma. It had been there all the time, but was undetected until the Spirit gave the word of wisdom.

Peter's recognition of the deceit of Ananias and Sapphira and the Spirit's disclosure to him of the presence of Cornelius' emissaries seem to be manifestations of the word of knowledge (5:3; 10:19, 20). I would like to suggest also that the word of knowledge can be recognized in Peter's sermon at Pentecost. The Word of God is the source of all true knowledge. Peter suddenly knew "this is that" because the Spirit quickened his understanding of Joel's prophecy (2:16-21). He did not reach this conclusion through long and thoughtful study. It was spontaneous—the result of supernatural illumination. It appears to me it was a word of knowledge based on the Word of God.

Paul does *not* call the third gift of revelation "the gift of discernment." This passage is sometimes misquoted and taken to mean something completely foreign to what the gift really is—*discerning of spirits.*

This gift is the supernatural ability to distinguish between true and false inspiration. At Philippi Paul and Silas were followed by a young fortune-teller everywhere they went (16:16-18). She kept shouting: "These men are the servants of the most high God, which show unto us the way of salvation." What she said was true, but Paul discerned that it came from the wrong kind of spirit. Satan was using the girl to harass God's ministers and interfere with their preaching. Paul cast the evil spirit out of her and destroyed her powers of divination. This was the gift of discerning of spirits in action.

Gifts of Power

Every Christian has faith, or he would not be saved. The gift of faith, however, is a special kind of faith for special needs. It may be for healing, but it can also operate in other situations.

When Peter lifted the lame man to his feet there was obviously an extraordinary quickening of the apostle's faith (3:7). Stephen did "great wonders and miracles among the people" because he was "full of faith" (6:8). Is it not possible the gift of faith was also manifested through Stephen during the moments of his martyrdom? How else can we explain his glowing spiritual victory in such a crisis? (See Acts 7:55-60.) The Spirit also exercised *gifts* of healing through Peter and Stephen.

In addition to the gifts of healing, why does Paul list another gift which he calls "the working of miracles"? The *New American Standard Bible* gives an alternate rendering of "miracles" as "works of power" (Acts 19:11). Many of the healings and deliverances from demons recorded in Acts are called miracles (8:6, 7; 19:11, 12).

Perhaps the working of miracles involves situations of greater magnitude. Raising the dead would surely be in this category (9:36-41). Jesus' miracles included other works of power besides healing. The temporary blinding of Elymas might be considered a miracle of judgment (13:8-12). Scriptural examples seem to indicate the gifts of faith, healing, and miracles often blend together until it is not easy to separate them into neat compartments.

Gifts of Utterance

These gifts are inspired speech prompted by the Holy Spirit. Prophecy and interpretation of tongues are in one's own language, but tongues are in a language unknown to the speaker.

In the Old Testament, prophecy often foretold the future, but not always. Prophets were also sent to comfort God's people in seasons of trouble and to rebuke them for their sins and lethargy when they strayed.

The predictive element is still present at times in prophecy, for the Spirit used Agabus to warn of a famine and to prepare Paul for his coming imprisonment (11:27, 28; 21:10, 11). According to 1 Corinthians 14:3, however, the New Testament prophet's message is more frequently for "edification, and exhortation, and comfort."

We are told in Acts 15:32: "Judas and Silas, being prophets also themselves, exhorted the brethren with many words, and confirmed them." "To confirm" is to support or strengthen. It is easy to understand why the Holy Spirit, through Paul, stresses the value of prophecy to the Church.

Another function of prophecy is mentioned in 1 Timothy 4:14. Paul indicates there was a prophetic utterance over Timothy concerning a spiritual gift the Lord gave him at his ordination. The apostle had referred to this earlier in the letter (1 Timothy 1:18). What appears to be a similar manifestation of prophecy is found in Acts 13:2. Paul and Barnabas were sent on their first missionary journey after "the Holy Ghost said." This indicates an utterance of the Spirit through human lips.

A word of caution should be added here. Some who have attempted to impart spiritual gifts and give other forms of direction to fellow Christians have done so in their own zeal without the Spirit's anointing. We must always be willing to have our spiritual manifestations tested by the Word and by the judgment of mature Christians. This is confirmed by the safeguard laid down in 1 Corinthians 14:29: "Let the prophets speak two or three, and let the other judge." The Greek word for "judge" means "to discriminate." It is closely related to the Greek word for "discerning" where the Word speaks of "discerning of spirits" in 1 Corinthians 12:10.

We do not find examples in Acts of the gift of interpretation of tongues. When tongues occur in Acts its function is the sign of the Spirit's infilling rather than a gift exercised in a meeting. Anyone who has been in Pentecostal services, however, has witnessed the manifestation of tongues with the interpretation. The interpretation, of course, is given supernaturally to the believer who ministers as an interpreter. According to 1 Corinthians 14:5 these gifts together are edifying to the church. Paul also refers to the exercise of tongues in private worship and prayer, which is edifying to the spirit of the individual (1 Corinthians 14:2, 4, 14, 15).

Through Paul, the Holy Spirit placed limitations on the public exercise of prophecy and tongues (1 Corinthians 14:27-33). These gifts are not to be put above Scripture and must always be consistent with its teachings. The Word alone is our infallible standard and guide. It has priority over all gifts in determining God's will and the course of our lives.

If we feel we have received an utterance from the Spirit while the Word is being ministered, none of its force will be lost by our waiting until the preaching or teaching of the Word is concluded. To interrupt the Word would create the confusion to which Paul refers in 1 Corinthians 14:33. Our responsibility for self-control is emphasized in verse 32. "Decently and in order" was, and is, the divine rule concerning all spiritual manifestations.

Other Gifts

At first it might seem strange that Paul calls the ministries of service, teaching, exhortation, giving, governing, mercy, and helps "gifts" (Romans 12:6-8; 1 Corinthians 12:28). By their very nature they are not as striking in their operation as some of the others. They blend into the daily routine of the church's work. But are not spiritual gifts as necessary under "ordinary" circumstances as in moments of crisis? Being somewhat inconspicuous does not make these gifts less vital.

To minister is to serve. Wouldn't you say this gift of service operated through the seven men appointed to distribute food to the widows? (See Acts 6:1-7.) Paul wrote about some Christians who addicted themselves to the ministry of the saints (1 Corinthians 16:15). What an addiction! There are Christians, God bless them, in whom the gift of service is constantly demonstrated. By the Spirit's anointing they know just where to fit in and do what is needed.

Some may have natural abilities that make them good teachers, but they will be more effective if the spiritual gift of teaching operates through them. Paul was not content to get people saved and leave them without a strong foundation for their faith. Who can doubt the gift of teaching flowed through him during those 18 months in Corinth (Acts 18:11) and throughout his ministry?

The gifts of exhortation and prophecy seem related and may sometimes be indistinguishable. To exhort is to comfort, console, and encourage. Barnabas must have been used by the Spirit in the ministry of this gift, for he was nicknamed "Son of Encouragement" (Acts 4:36, *NASB*).

It may be surprising to hear of the gift of giving. All

Christians should give, but there are some who seem to excel in this ministry. Again I think of Barnabas. When he sold his property he brought the money and gave it gladly to the church (4:37). Ananias and Sapphira gave some of their money too, but with a different spirit (5:1, 2).

"He that ruleth, with diligence" (Romans 12:8). This corresponds to the "governments" of 1 Corinthians 12:28. God's work requires leadership. Under the Spirit's direction Paul organized churches and appointed leaders. He laid down qualifications for them in his epistles. Men not qualified by the Spirit for leadership in the church are unwise to try to assume it.

The Spirit clearly exercised the gift of government through all of the apostles, including Paul. This is true also of the elders who were given the care of local congregations (Acts 14:23).

"He that showeth mercy, with cheerfulness," (Romans 12:8) refers to acts of mercy. It means help and assistance given to those in need. What would our churches be like if it were not for dear saints through whom the Spirit manifests this gift? They shun personal glory. Often they work unnoticed behind the scenes; yet they sustain many hearts. Paul mentions one of these, Phoebe, in Romans 16:1, 2. This gift is connected closely with the gift of service. Dorcas was surely one through whom the Spirit exercised both (Acts 9:36, 39).

In 1 Corinthians 12:28 Paul identifies two other gifts not included in verses 8-10. We have already mentioned "governments"; the other is "helps." Not everyone is a leader, but every leader needs helpers. When Paul and Silas traveled together, Paul was always in the foreground but Silas was by his side. It takes grace to play second fiddle. Silas was a man who could do it without resentment. The Spirit qualified this noble laborer by manifesting through him the gift of helps.

Needed for the Body

Paul compares the Church to a human body. Each part, no matter how ordinary it seems, has a function to perform for the well-being of the whole. When the body must work, the hands reach out to perform the activity. The feet provide the mobility. The eyes and ears gather information and transmit it to the brain for evaluation. These members also detect danger. The nose warns of odors that may come from a source perilous to health.

Members of the body are sometimes called on to defend one another, as when the hands fly up in front of the face to ward off a flying object. Occasionally the feet must protect the whole body by carrying it to safety.

The gifts of the Holy Spirit have much the same function in the Church as the various members have in the body. The Church needs knowledge and direction, awareness of danger, and protection from foes that seek to hinder or destroy it. It must distinguish between what is deadly and what is wholesome; between the false and the true.

In Acts we see these various needs arising in the Church and note the Spirit's timely exercise of the appropriate gifts.

10

They Wore the Mantle

The Early Church's Leadership

As He has done ever since, God cast the mantle of leadership on chosen individuals in the Early Church. We will make several references in this chapter to the Epistles to fill in details omitted in Acts. Our limited space will not permit the use of every Scripture passage mentioning these leaders. I suggest you check your concordance for other passages.

Peter

Each of the apostles was a leader, but Luke's Book of 28 short chapters is not long enough to tell about all of them.

Despite his shortcomings, Peter had natural qualities of leadership and the Holy Spirit used and polished them. During the waiting time before Pentecost, who called a business meeting to elect Judas' replacement? That's right. It was Peter (Acts 1:15-22). Who thundered the message of the risen, ascended Christ to the multitude? Peter, of course. What a changed man this was! The night of Jesus' arrest he had dodged, evaded, shrank back, and cringed. Now he was "standing up" (1:15; 2:14).

When the crowd was amazed at the healing of the lame man, Peter did what is typical of men truly filled with the Spirit. He strenuously disclaimed any glory for himself and quickly directed attention to Christ (3:12-16).

When the Jewish authorities seized Peter and John after this miracle, "They took knowledge of them, that they had been with Jesus" (4:13). What an encouragement to those of us who have failed. A few weeks earlier Peter had been engulfed in the midnight darkness of despair because he had denied his Lord. Could he ever rise again? Oh yes, and what a comeback! Jesus' influence on his life was apparent even to his enemies.

Peter was the man Jesus chose to open the gospel door to the Gentiles (Matthew 16:18). That he had been a devout observer of the Law is clear from his statement during his vision on the rooftop (Acts 10:13, 14). Peter was not alone in his feelings about Gentiles. The mark of a big man, and especially a Spirit-filled man, is his willingness to admit mistakes and change his thinking.

When Peter heard from the Spirit that he was to take Christ's message to a Gentile home in Caesarea he submitted (10:19-23). As he witnessed the outpouring of the Spirit on Cornelius' household, he was quick to understand what God was doing (10:44-48). At the council in Jerusalem he sided vigorously with the leaders who saw the error of trying to hang the Law around the necks of Gentile Christians (15:7-11). Peter had already been questioned about his trip to Caesarea, but did not flinch in the presence of brethren who lacked his enlightenment (11:1-18).

The man who had punctuated his denials of Jesus with cursing showed no fear when cruel Herod jailed him for the obvious purpose of making him another martyr (12:1-17).

After the council in chapter 15 we read no more in Acts about Peter. The Spirit turns our attention to Paul, the apostle to the Gentiles. We do, of course, have Peter's two letters in the New Testament. They are short, but packed with inspiration.

In Galatians 2:11-14 Paul refers to an incident involving Peter that is not mentioned in Acts. Most scholars place it during the period covered by Acts 15:30-35. Although the Jerusalem council decreed that converted Gentiles did not have to keep the Law, some apparently felt the Jewish Christians still had these obligations. When a number of these people came from Jerusalem to Antioch, Peter's former courage did a sudden disappearing act. The fellowship he had been enjoying with the Gentile believers came to a halt. This shocking cowardice brought a sharp public rebuke from Paul. If Peter harbored any bitterness over it, such feelings did not last, for in his second epistle he wrote of "our beloved brother Paul" (2 Peter 3:15).

James, The Brother of John

Three leaders named James were in the Early Church. The second James among the 12 apostles was the son of Alpheus (Matthew 10:3). James number three was "the Lord's brother" (Galatians 1:19). He was not one of the Twelve, yet he became a prominent leader (Acts 15:13).

James the brother of John had his life cut short by martyrdom at the hands of Herod. He was the first apostle to die for his Lord (Acts 12:1, 2). Peter, James, and John had been partners in the fishing business (Luke 5:10). They were with Jesus on some wonderful occasions when the others were not. The most notable was the Saviour's transfiguration (Matthew 17:1, 2). Some call this trio the "inner circle."

During the early days of the Church we read of Peter and John being together, but for some reason James seemed to drop out of the circle. His time of service was brief, but it seems appropriate to include his name among the leaders because of his prominence during Jesus' earthly ministry.

John

Probably the first work of John that comes to our minds is his incomparable Gospel, with its tremendous testimony to the deity of Jesus Christ. He also wrote three Epistles—two of them very short. Then there is that great prophetic Book, Revelation—the result of John's visions during his imprisonment on Patmos. His writings have an interesting variety.

John was much in Peter's company after Pentecost. They were on their way to prayer when the lame man was healed. The Jerusalem church sent the two of them to pray for the Samaritan converts to receive the Holy Spirit (Acts 8:14 17). This is the last record of John in Acts.

The transformation of John from a "son of thunder" (Mark 3:17) is evident in his first epistle, where the theme of love is dominant. John's devotion to his Lord is underscored by his leaning on His breast at the Last Supper (John 13:25; 21:20). The dying Saviour entrusted the care of His mother to John (John 19:26, 27). Perhaps this is one of the best evidences of the kind of man he was.

James, The Lord's Brother

Although Luke does not state directly which

James he is referring to in Acts 12:17, 15:13, and 21:18, many Bible scholars believe it is the Lord's brother and not the son of Alpheus. The attempts of some to make him Jesus' cousin and identify him and the second James as the same person seem strained.

As one of the Lord's brothers, James was an unbeliever in Him at first (John 7:3-5). We are not told when his conversion took place, but he was probably the James to whom Paul refers as one of the earliest witnesses to Christ's resurrection (1 Corinthians 15:7).

Jesus' brethren were in the Upper Room (Acts 1:14), and this would have included James. Paul considered him one of the church's important leaders, for he and Peter were the only two he saw when he returned to Jerusalem after his 3 years in Arabia (Galatians 1:19).

James and Peter appear to have had a close relationship. When he was delivered from prison by the angel, Peter was anxious that the good news be conveyed quickly to James (12:17). Paul calls James, Peter, and John (in that order) the men who "seemed to be pillars" of the church (Galatians 2:9). From an unbeliever to a pillar—another testimony to the transforming power of Christ!

Paul says the men whose visit produced Peter's unfortunate conduct "came from James" (Galatians 2:12). We cannot be certain James sent them to check up on the Jewish Christians in Antioch. This verse may indicate only they were from the Jerusalem church, of which James was the overseer. It would be disappointing if James was trying to keep Jewish believers under the bondage from which he, by the Spirit's direction, had released the Gentiles. There seems to be no direct proof, however, that he had such intentions.

We have a New Testament Epistle written by James, who identifies himself only as "a servant of God." The traditional view is its author is James, the Lord's brother. The sound, practical teaching of the Epistle testifies that the Spirit's wisdom was still flowing through this man.

Stephen

Stephen's name first appears as one of the seven chosen in Acts 6. His career was short, but who wouldn't be glad to leave behind a record like Stephen's? He was full of faith (6:5, 8). His conduct before his accusers (Acts 7) was a ringing testimony to the peace and mental stability the Spirit gives in times of trial.

Even when his tormentors gnashed their teeth at him in blind rage, Stephen was full of the Holy Spirit (7:54, 55). He had the honor of being the first Christian to wear the martyr's crown. The ascended Lord himself rose and stood before His throne to welcome him home (7:55, 56). Only a man full of the Spirit of God could pray, with his dying breath, "Lay not this sin to their charge," (7:60).

Acts 8:1 tells us Saul was one who cast his vote for Stephen's death. We will say more about this in the next chapter. Did Stephen's shining face haunt Saul's memory? I find it easy to believe it did.

Philip

Like Stephen, Philip was chosen to "serve tables," but he was more than a foreman in the grocery warehouse. He too had a fruitful preaching ministry. When many of the Christians were driven from Jerusalem by persecution, Philip joined them. His first stop was Samaria, where God sent a great revival

(8:4-25). Yet when he was ordered to leave the meeting and go to the desert, he responded without hesitation (8:26-40). Who knows how far the influence of the gospel spread because Philip led an Ethiopian official to Christ? Verses 29 and 30 give an insight into the kind of man he was: "The Spirit said . . . and Philip ran."

Philip could not board a jet to travel to his meetings, but on one occasion the Lord gave him even faster transportation (8:39). Usually he didn't get to stay long in one place. Verse 40 tells us his tour covered many cities.

In Acts 21:8 he is called "Philip the evangelist." He was a family man with "four daughters, virgins, which did prophesy" (21:9). This underscores his spiritual influence in his own home. On this occasion Philip was entertaining Paul and his traveling party, including Luke. He was a man of hospitality as well as faith.

Barnabas

This "son of encouragement," a Levite from Cyprus, is one of my favorite people in Acts. Liberality with his finances is one of the first of his good traits we notice (4:36, 37).

When the Christians were afraid to welcome the newly converted Saul, it was Barnabas who reassured them the former persecutor's experience was genuine (9:26, 27). Barnabas "was a good man, and full of the Holy Ghost and of faith" (11:24). What better preacher could have been sent to encourage the new converts at Antioch (11:25, 26)?

Barnabas and Paul were chosen by the Holy Spirit to launch a far-reaching missionary campaign (13:2). The two of them had previously carried gifts from the Antioch congregation to the Jerusalem church after the Spirit had warned them of a coming famine (11:27-30). Although he was not one of the original 12, Barnabas was called an apostle (14:14). He was also a prophet and/or teacher (13:1).

The human side of both Barnabas and Paul comes through loud and clear in their clash over taking Barnabas' cousin Mark on another journey. "Barnabas determined. . . . But Paul thought not good . . ." (15:37, 38). Neither man behaved gloriously, but both had their points. We can understand why Barnabas might have accused his partner of being harsh. We can sympathize with Paul if he felt Barnabas was more concerned about a relative's feelings than the success of their mission. At any rate, two committed servants of Christ became embroiled in strife that ruptured their partnership.

Barnabas and Paul separated, but the Lord still used both of them in His work. The fatherly Barnabas took Mark with him. Barnabas surely was a strong force in the younger man's eventual maturity. The former deserter became the writer of a Gospel. Who knows how much his character was shaped by the encouragement of this godly man?

Paul got a jolt when "Barnabas also" caved in under the pressure of the Antioch incident (Galatians 2:13). He was the last one from whom you would have expected such behavior. I do not see this lapse, however, as a major detraction from his character or the general tone and spirit of his life. Perhaps such instances are recorded to warn us that no Christian can afford to let down his guard.

Silas

Here is a man whose later ministry was under the

shadow of the powerful personality of Paul. He is generally identified as the Silvanus in Paul's epistles. In Acts 15:32 he is called a prophet. Silas was one of the men chosen to convey the council's decision to Antioch (15:22-35). His love for the church there was so great that he stayed for a time, along with Paul and Barnabas.

After his break with Barnabas, Paul chose Silas to take his place. This decision was undoubtedly in the will of God, for He made the two a mighty force in the spreading of the gospel. We have no record of dissension between Silas and Paul. They shared sufferings as well as victories, including that stirring night in the Philippian jail (16:19-40).

Peter called Silas "a faithful brother," and trusted him to deliver his first epistle to the dispersed Christians (1 Peter 5:12).

Apollos

Apollos is mentioned in only two passages in Acts (18:24-28; 19:1). Paul's references to him in his epistles, however, show he was an important leader.

Apollos would be called a pulpiteer today. He was one of those rare men who combined eloquence with profound scriptural knowledge and spiritual fervor. After Aquila and Priscilla "expounded unto him the way of God more perfectly," he had a powerful, Christ-exalting ministry among the Jews.

The impact of Apollos' ministry in Corinth is noted in Paul's reference to him in his first letter to that church (1 Corinthians 1:12; 3:4-6, 22; 4:6; 16:12). In these passages, as well as another reference in Titus 3:13, Paul's affection for Apollos is obvious.

How encouraging it is that God can use imperfect men to do His work!

11

God's Iron Man

Paul, The Early Church's
Missionary-Theologian

"And the witnesses laid down their clothes at a young man's feet, whose name was Saul.... And Saul was consenting unto his death" (Acts 7:58; 8:1).

This is our introduction to the man destined by God's grace to become Christianity's greatest champion. Because of his prominence in Acts and his calling as the apostle to the Gentiles, I feel compelled to devote a chapter to Paul rather than a few paragraphs in considering the Early Church's leadership. He is introduced by his Hebrew name *Saul*. We are more familiar with his Roman name *Paul*, used by Luke after Acts 13:9. We'll start with "Saul," then switch to "Paul" after his conversion.

In consenting to Stephen's martyrdom, Saul had joined in a decision reached among the Jewish leaders. Knowing his fierce hatred of the church, we can be sure his vote was wholehearted. Acts 26:10 indicates Saul had been a leader in the Jewish hierarchy and worked closely with them in their persecution of the Christians.

Saul was proud of his hometown of Tarsus (21:39). Many of his youthful years, however, had been spent in Jerusalem as a student of Gamaliel. Under this teacher he had been rigidly instructed in the law of Moses (22:3). The eagerness with which young Saul had absorbed this teaching is noted in his statement to Agrippa: "After the most straitest sect of our religion I lived a Pharisee" (26:5).

At no time after his conversion did Paul scorn his upbringing. He gladly declared that his father was also a Pharisee (23:6). He was anxious that the Jews in Rome know he was not a traitor to his heritage (28:17). He always insisted his preaching was in complete accord with the message of the Hebrew prophets and the teaching of Moses (26:22). But until Saul met Christ his fervent devotion to Judaism had fueled a smoldering hatred of the Christian church. Finally it burst into irrational violence. His testimony before Agrippa reveals that Stephen was not the only Christian for whose death Saul had voted in the Sanhedrin. "Exceedingly mad against them" was his own description of his abhorrence of the followers of Jesus (26:10, 11). No pity was stirred in Saul even if the Christian was a woman. He filled the prisons with every believer he could lay his hands on (22:4).

Saul was driven by an unswerving conviction that his campaign of terror was a service to God. He saw this new religion as a threat to his beloved Judaism. Stephen's death seemed to whet his appetite for more blood. Like a madman, "he made havoc of the church, entering into every house, and haling men and women committed them to prison" (8:3). Acts 9:1 sounds like a bloodthirsty animal panting after its prey: "And Saul, yet breathing out threatenings and slaughter. . . ."

What trembling Christian, in hiding or on his way to martyrdom through the efforts of Saul, could dream this man would soon become a Christian himself? Miracles abound in Acts, but none surpasses the conversion of this raging persecutor.

Stopped in His Tracks

If Saul's conversion experience seems to have been rather violent, it only matched his rampage against the Church. Like a bounty hunter, he hurried to Damascus to bring more Christians to trial at Jerusalem. The one thing he wasn't counting on was intervention by heaven. Then suddenly—the light, the fall, the Voice. And his life was turned around.

Paul later described the light from heaven as "above the brightness of the sun" (26:13). Yet it was not nearly so bright as the light that would soon be shining in his soul.

What a revolution! Saul had been breathing out threatenings and slaughter. Now he fell to the earth, trembling and astonished (9:1, 4, 6). When he finally got up he had to be led by the hand (9:8). God knows how to bring down a proud man quickly!

The voice Saul heard called him by name and asked a question that startled him: "Saul, Saul, why persecutest thou me?" (v. 4). Things were happening too fast for the stricken Pharisee to comprehend. "Whom am I persecuting? Who is speaking?" And then the reply that turned the fire of hatred into the unquenchable flame of love: "I am Jesus." Saul thought he had been persecuting Christians. But Jesus said, "When you lash out against My people your blows fall on Me."

How quickly the iron will of Saul submitted: "Lord, what wilt thou have me to do?" He had been giving orders, but now he was learning to take them.

The answer did not come immediately. He would

have to go into the city and wait to be told of his next move. The headstrong Saul would be "told"?

As he groped for hands to lead him, he knew things would never be the same. His blindness lasted 3 days. They were days of fasting for Saul. Food and drink seemed unimportant. He needed time to think and meditate; to absorb the events that had suddenly exploded upon him.

We are told nothing about Ananias whom God sent to Saul. He is identified only as "a certain disciple" (9:10). He had heard plenty about this fanatical Sanhedrin member. His heart must have trembled as he wondered where the next blow would fall. Ananias was the first Christian to learn the arrester had been arrested. He was also the first to hear the great commission the Lord gave Saul: "He is a chosen vessel unto me, to bear my name before the Gentiles, and kings, and the children of Israel" (9:15).

What a far-reaching ministry Paul would have— Gentiles, kings, Israelites. He was a testimony to the fact that God does not despise natural ability or formal training. On the contrary, He uses them when they are committed to Him. Paul's background gave him the ear of audiences with whom others would have had no rapport.

Paul's career would not be all glamor. There were "great things" to be suffered in the service of Christ (9:16). The Lord knows who is equal to such tests. Paul's disciplined life, plus the unfailing grace of God, made him more than a conqueror when he met Satan's heavy attacks.

What a privilege for Ananias to be the one who laid his hands on the man soon to be Paul the apostle. The Lord knew who to send on that mission. Luke could not spend long telling us about this dear Christian.

Perhaps in heaven we will have opportunity to ask Ananias some questions about that momentous day in Damascus.

In the Service of Christ

Paul's preaching began "straightway." His theme was what it would always be—Jesus is the Christ, the Son of God (9:20).

Paul's burden for his own people took him into the synagogues with his Christian witness. The impact of his ministry is clear: "But Saul increased the more in strength, and confounded the Jews which dwelt at Damascus, proving that this is very Christ" (9:22). How did Paul do this "proving"? The way he would do it throughout his ministry—by the Scriptures. The Holy Spirit was using Paul's store of knowledge of the Old Testament. Day after day He unfolded truths to him from the Scriptures he had read so often. The scales had fallen from Paul's spiritual eyes just as they had from his physical eyes (9:18). How clearly he now saw that Jesus is the fulfillment of the Law and the theme of the prophets.

Luke does not tell us of Paul's retirement to Arabia, but Paul wrote about it (Galatians 1:15-17). It is generally believed that during this time of solitude Paul received from God many of the revelations he unfolded in his epistles.

It is not easy to mesh the chronology of events in Acts 9:19-28 with Paul's account in Galatians. Bible scholars are not all in agreement about the time of the Jerusalem visit and the retreat to Arabia. I will not pursue the matter further, but there is no reason to consider it a serious problem.

Luke does not tell us the number of the "many days" of Acts 9:23. We do know the man who had headed for Damascus expecting to leave with a multitude of Christian prisoners left instead as a fugitive under cover of darkness. From the top of the city wall he was lowered in a basket—now the hunted instead of the hunter (9:23-25). But he left a happy man instead of a tormented one.

How could Paul forget Barnabas' role in making a place for him among the Christians in Jerusalem (9:26-28)? Barnabas was also responsible for Paul's association with the church at Antioch. The Jerusalem church had sent Barnabas there after they learned of the great revival. Guided no doubt by the Holy Spirit, Barnabas went to Paul's hometown of Tarsus and brought him to the church (11:19-26). Antioch was to become one of the most prominent congregations of the Apostolic Era. There can be no doubt about Paul's contribution to its spiritual stability and growth.

The Call to Other Fields

It was during Paul's stay in Antioch that the Holy Spirit commissioned Barnabas and him for a great outreach into untouched fields (13:2). Their strategy followed a pattern that had undoubtedly been impressed on them by the Spirit. When there was a synagogue in a city, that was where they went first (13:5). Paul's sermon in the synagogue of another Antioch (in Pisidia) shows how he built on the Old Testament truths with which his Jewish audiences were familiar. Always he moved on to the great focal point of those Scriptures—Jesus, God's Christ.

Not surprisingly there was usually a mixed reaction from the congregations of the synagogues (13:44, 45). Paul's training as a rabbi gave him an attentive audience. The trouble erupted when he

106

reached the climax of his message and declared Jesus to be the Son of God and only Saviour.

At Lystra the people called Paul "Mercurius" (Mercury) because he was the chief speaker (14:12). This is rather surprising, for others seemed to think he was a better writer than speaker (2 Corinthians 10:10). If the latter assessment was true, it should encourage all other poor speakers, for God used Paul's "contemptible" speech to shake an empire.

How many of us could get up and start preaching again after being knocked unconscious by a barrage of stones (Acts 14:19-21)? Paul knew how to draw both spiritual and physical strength from the Lord to whose work he was absolutely committed. He was also a man of iron self-discipline (1 Corinthians 9:25-27). His own discomfort, inconvenience, and suffering were of little concern to him. A man of less tenacity would have been unequal to the battles he fought.

We have already noted Paul's great role in the Jerusalem council. How amazing that a man who had lived and breathed the Law from his youth should become famous for his preaching of salvation by grace through faith apart from the works of the Law!

A Call in the Night

Does it come as a surprise that even a man of Paul's spiritual stature had times of uncertainty about God's will? Twice the pressure of the Spirit in his soul stopped him from going where he had been headed (Acts 16:6, 7). Finally God's direction came through a vision at night (16:9, 10). Paul and his company were to take the message of Christ to Europe.

Why hadn't this vision come to Paul in the beginning? Why the time of uncertainty when his moves were halted? Could this not have been further discipline, a test of his obedience? Even apostles need such schooling at times.

From Acts 15:40 on it is no longer Paul and Barnabas; it is Paul and Silas. Their trip to Europe produced fruit immediately (16:14, 15). It also brought them a night in prison! No warden ever had such prisoners as these two. Instead of cursing about their bleeding backs and shackled feet, they sang praises to God—at midnight. "The prisoners heard them," but it was soon evident Someone else did too (16:25, 26). These men were marching under orders from the Supreme Commander of the universe, and how He responded to their songs! The earth shook.

The jailer feared a mass escape when he heard all the cell doors clanging open. Only Paul's quick cry saved the man from suicide. Before the night was over, the jailer and his household were part of the family of God (16:27-34).

It is refreshing to note the difference in personalities among the Early Church leaders. Peter was just plain, uncomplicated Peter, but Paul was a more complex character. Some probably called him stern and inflexible. Yet his heart broke over the weeping of his friends at Caesarea (21:13). He spoke unashamedly of his own tears (20:19, 31). He was so full of tenderness toward his fellow Jews that he would have sacrificed his own soul to save them (Romans 9:3).

The Spirit did not try to make the Church's leaders carbon copies of one another. He used each one the way he came out of his own mold. Naturally He worked at refining them, just as He does with us. You cannot read 2 Timothy without sensing Paul's mellowing. Can you imagine how Mark felt when

Timothy told him, "Paul wants you again, Mark. He says you're profitable to him for the ministry" (2 Timothy 4:11)?

Finishing His Course

When Paul was arrested and appeared before Roman officials he had one defense: He simply told the story of how he had met Jesus (Acts 26:1-20). The testimony of his conversion was the only defense he offered before the howling mob in Jerusalem (22:1-16).

When Paul was heading for Jerusalem for the last time, into what he knew would be certain trouble, he told the Ephesian elders his only concern was finishing his course (20:24). He saw the Christian life as a race. He was determined not to be one who started, only to drop out along the way. But he didn't intend to stumble across the finish line with a final desperate gasp. He wanted to break the tape with a shout of joy, and he did.

We must read the Epistles for many of the details of Paul's life. The Book of Acts closes with him as Rome's prisoner under rather mild conditions. For 2 years he was permitted to maintain "his own hired house." Of course he was under the supervision of a Roman soldier. He was not as free as he had been before his arrest, but he was allowed to receive visitors and tell them of Christ.

Luke condenses the activity of those 2 years into the last two verses of his Book. What we see Paul doing was the very heart of his ministry until he won the martyr's crown: "Teaching those things which concern the Lord Jesus Christ" (Acts 28:31).

12

Command Posts

Local Congregations of the Early Church

During the great land battles of World War II the nerve center was the supreme headquarters of the theater of war where the action was. From there a stream of orders went out to commanders in the field. The latter had some flexibility to meet changing situations, but major strategy originated at the supreme headquarters.

Close to the battle lines on each front was another headquarters. It was much smaller, but absolutely vital. This was the command post where the officer responsible for that phase of the operations directed his troops from close range. The commander's responsibility was to carry out the orders from the general at the top.

The Church's orders come from heaven, but the local church is the command post. Here is where the real battles are fought. What strengthens the local church advances the work of Christ. What weakens the local church is detrimental to the Lord's cause.

Most of the churches established in the early days are not named in Acts. We know there were many, and that the number grew rapidly: "And so were the churches established in the faith, and increased in number daily" (16:5).

Jesus declared He would build a Church. It would not be a formless monolith. The stones from which this living Temple is being constructed are redeemed lives (Ephesians 2:19-22). Throughout the centuries these Blood-washed saints have come together in local congregations to worship and work and carry out the Great Commission. Let's look at the churches Luke mentions in Acts.

Jerusalem

This was the first local church. It sprang into being on the Day of Pentecost and grew by leaps and bounds thereafter.

Even after the number of churches multiplied, Jerusalem was still the hub. When many Christians left because of persecution, the apostles remained (8:1). The influence of the church was strong in the city, but it had its conflicts with the Jewish authorities.

It was natural that new churches should look to Jerusalem for support and guidance. The leaders there exerted a strong influence on the work in other areas. Their concern for the churches in outlying regions was deep. The journey of Peter and John to Samaria is an example. It was not a private venture; they were sent by the apostolic group (8:14).

When the apostles learned many had found Christ in Antioch through the ministry of dispersed Christians, they sent Barnabas. They knew it was not enough to win people to Christ, for they must be instructed and guided afterward (11:22-24).

At some time after his conversion Paul went to Jerusalem. He was careful to explain to the Galatians

111

that he did not go there immediately, for he wanted them to know his teaching came from the Lord and he was not merely parroting the other apostles (Galatians 1:15-19). Obviously, though, Paul wanted to establish a relationship with the Jerusalem church and its leadership.

The Jerusalem church had a harder time than the other churches breaking away from Jewish religious practices after Pentecost. The Christians continued to worship in their beloved temple while carrying on their own services from house to house (Acts 2:46; 3:1; 5:20, 25, 42). We learn from these passages that they boldly carried their witness for Christ into the temple.

Antioch

When the Christians who were driven from Jerusalem reached Antioch they preached only to Jews (11:19). Later men who came from Cyprus and Cyrene ministered to the Gentiles, who eagerly received Christ in large numbers (11:20, 21). The labor of the evangelists was followed by the strong work of the teacher Barnabas. Lest anyone imagine a teacher's work cannot be evangelistic, we should note that during Barnabas' ministry "much people was added unto the Lord" (11:24).

What church enjoyed the ministry of greater preachers than Antioch? Barnabas saw a need for Paul's type of ministry in the growing congregation and brought him to Antioch for a whole year (11:25, 26). Later there were others who joined the ministerial staff for a time.

It was at Antioch the name *Christians* was first attached to the followers of Jesus. This tells us something about their testimony in their community. *Christ* was the first part of the name by which outsiders decided to identify them.

The relationship between the Jerusalem and Antioch churches was deep. The latter congregation lost no time sending help to Jerusalem in time of famine. Jerusalem had ministered to them in spiritual things. Now they were applying Paul's principle of ministering to the mother church in material things (Romans 15:27).

Antioch became a church where God based some of the great leaders until He was ready to send them on a mission:

> Now there were in the church that was at Antioch certain prophets and teachers; as Barnabas, and Simeon that was called Niger, and Lucius of Cyrene, and Manaen, which had been brought up with Herod the tetrarch, and Saul (Acts 13:1).

Isn't it amazing that Herod Antipas' foster brother was one of this group?

Barnabas and Saul soon answered the Spirit's summons to "the work whereunto [He had] called them" (13:2). Antioch was still their home base to which they returned to report God's blessings on their ministry (14:26-28).

Antioch's importance among the early churches is seen in the delivery there of the official letter from Jerusalem after the council (15:30). The ministry of Silas was soon added to that of others (15:34).

The church must have been sorrowful over the break between Paul and Barnabas. Yet they gave Paul and his new partner Silas a prayerful send-off as they began their missionary journey (15:40).

Thessalonica

At Thessalonica Paul followed his custom of preaching first to the Jews in their synagogue (17:1-3). As usual there was a division among his listeners. Those who opposed him did not do so passively. They found wicked men who were eager to join a mob and start a riot. Two accusations were hurled at Paul and his companions: (1) they had turned the world upside down; and (2) they were saying there is another king named Jesus, thus encouraging disloyalty to Caesar. The uproar was so violent it seemed advisable for Paul and Silas to make a hasty departure to Beroea at night (17:1-10).

Christianity has made its greatest strides in times of severe opposition. The riot at Thessalonica only added fuel to the revival fires, and a strong church was established. Along with the believing Jews the original congregation consisted of Gentiles and prominent women. This nucleus was not a tiny handful; it was large (17:4).

Paul later wrote two letters to the Thessalonian church. From the first one we learn of that congregation's far-reaching influence:

> So that ye were ensamples to all that believe in Macedonia and Achaia. For from you sounded out the word of the Lord not only in Macedonia and Achaia, but also in every place your faith to God-ward is spread abroad; so that we need not to speak any thing" (1 Thessalonians 1:7, 8).

Those Christians were following the lead of the church's founder in turning their world upside down. The truth is, of course, they were turning it rightside up!

Beroea

The account of this church's beginning is brief, but what is said about the Bereans bears repeating. How many Bible classes have taken their name from this church? They became noted for searching the Scriptures to discover if the preaching they heard was true (Acts 17:10, 11). Influential Greek women were a part of this congregation (v. 12).

The aggressive Jews at Thessalonica would give Paul and Silas no rest; they soon followed them to Beroea. They were masters at creating disturbances. Since Paul was their chief target it seemed best for him to leave, although Silas and Timothy stayed until Paul sent for them from Athens (17:13-15).

When Paul left Ephesus for Macedonia and Greece, one of his companions was a man from Beroea named Sopater (20:4). The work of the Lord in that city was moving on.

Corinth

After Paul's brief stay in Athens he came to Corinth, a city notorious for its immorality. It was a prosperous commercial center, which made it a strategic location for another church. We are soon introduced to a couple who became very close to Paul—Aquila and Priscilla. They were tentmakers like Paul and had been exiled from Rome by the emperor's anti-Semitic campaign. They opened their home to the apostle and the three worked at their trade; with Paul taking the Christian message to the synagogue every Sabbath. After a time Silas and Timothy rejoined Paul (18:1-5).

The predictable negative reaction to Paul's preaching came from most of the Jews, leading him to declare that he would turn his ministry to the Gentiles. Providentially he was able to carry on his work in a house next door to the synagogue. The president of the synagogue turned to Christ and the revival was on (18:7, 8).

Paul stayed in Corinth for more than 1½ years, after receiving a reassuring message from the Lord in a vision. When he left for Ephesus he was accompanied by his good friends Aquila and Priscilla (18:9-18).

The eloquent Apollos paid a visit to Corinth and was mightily used of the Lord. His ministry was especially effective among the Jews, who were led through his preaching to see that Jesus is the Messiah to whom the Old Testament witnessed (18:24 to 19:1).

This church had its problems, as we learn from Paul's two letters to them. He called them carnal babies for their division over the men who had preached to them (1 Corinthians 3:1-4). The immoral atmosphere of the city had seeped into the congregation (1 Corinthians 5). Church members sued each other in court (1 Corinthians 6:1-8). Their understanding of the function of spiritual gifts had become distorted (1 Corinthians 12; 14). False apostles undermined Paul's influence among some of the Corinthians after he left (2 Corinthians 11).

No, there was not perfection in those early churches. The Corinthians seemed to cause Paul more heartache than any other group. But he loved them anyway and closed his second letter with these words: "The grace of the Lord Jesus Christ, and the love of God, and the communion of the Holy Ghost, be with you all. Amen" (2 Corinthians 13:14).

Ephesus

After Paul left Corinth his travels eventually took him to Ephesus. He did not stay long this time. Leaving Aquila and Priscilla there, he visited many churches before returning (Acts 18:18 to 19:1).

One of his first experiences in Ephesus was with a small group of disciples who had heard only part of the truth. When Paul explained to them that John the Baptist's ministry had been simply an introduction to the work of Christ, they quickly responded. After Paul baptized them in water they were filled with the Holy Spirit. Undoubtedly this company of 12 became part of the church that was established in the city (19:1-7).

Paul had not abandoned the Jews. At Ephesus he went to the synagogue and was allowed to preach there for 3 months before signs of trouble led him to change locations. Through his daily preaching in a schoolroom for 2 years, the message of Christ was spread throughout Asia Minor (19:9, 10).

Ephesus was the scene of a huge bonfire where many new Christians publicly burned their occult books. It was also where the silversmiths who made shrines for the false goddess Diana created an up-roar. But despite opposition, the victory of the gospel in that great city is summarized in these words: "So mightily grew the word of God and prevailed" (19:20).

Paul's epistle to the Ephesians is one of the jewels of the New Testament. Something of the spirit of this church is revealed in Jesus' commendation of them in Revelation 2:1-7. They were a busy, hard-working congregation, quick to discern error, intolerant of evil, and patient in suffering. It is unfortunate that our Lord also had to rebuke them for leaving their first love. This, of course, is a danger against which all of us must guard.

The affection between Paul and the Ephesian church is seen in an incident during his last trip to Jerusalem. He wanted to have a final visit with the leaders of the congregation. He sent for them and they lost no time in coming. A tearful farewell followed. The elders from Ephesus went with Paul as far as they could as they accompanied him to his ship. Their hearts broke as they realized they would see him no more in this world. I find their loyalty to the man who was the spiritual father of their church most inspiring (Acts 20:17-37).

Some Observations

Although the organization of the early churches was not complex, there was nothing disorganized about them. In Acts 14:23 we read of Paul and Barnabas ordaining elders in every church. The whole Church was under the umbrella of apostolic authority. One prominent characteristic of church operations in those days was order. This would have been impossible without authority. If anyone imagines that order and authority stifle growth, he should read the Book of Acts again.

Even during the church's internal problems there was order. This is evident during the food distribution crisis and the council meeting. Those business sessions were democratic, but controlled.

The apostles kept a close watch on everything that happened. When the others heard of Peter's visit to Cornelius they made an immediate investigation. Their beliefs needed correcting, but their motives were sincere. They felt they were attending to their proper business. When Peter told his story they agreed his mission to the Gentiles was the Lord's doing.

The apostles' authority came directly from Jesus, and the Christians were deeply aware of this. It was "the apostles' doctrine" they followed (2:42). Apostolic authority was demonstrated in Peter's handling of the Ananias and Sapphira incident. When the church had a common treasury for a time it was the apostles who were in charge of it (4:34-37).

Although the churches did not have the kind of communication we have today, frequent apostolic visits helped them feel close to one another. From Acts 9:32 it appears Peter made regular rounds of many of the churches. Paul carried on the same practice (15:36, 41; 18:22, 23).

13

How Shall They Hear?

Preaching in the Early Church

"How shall they hear without a preacher?" (Romans 10:14).

The Bible exalts the ministry of preaching. Jesus was a preacher (Matthew 4:17). To introduce Him to Israel, John the Baptist came preaching (Matthew 3:1).

Peter called Noah a "preacher of righteousness" (2 Peter 2:5). Paul said he was ordained a preacher as well as an apostle (1 Timothy 2:7; 2 Timothy 1:11).

In Titus 1:3 Paul wrote that God has "manifested his word through preaching." And he exhorted Timothy to preach the Word (2 Timothy 4:2). In this he was echoing the command of the Lord Jesus to His disciples: "As ye go, preach . . ." (Matthew 10:7).

Joel's prophecy, repeated by Peter, declares that when the Spirit is poured out on God's servants and handmaidens "they shall prophesy" (Acts 2:18). The message of redemption is proclaimed by men preaching under the anointing of the Holy Spirit. This gives true preaching a prophetic aspect. It sets it apart from the kind produced by human talent alone.

With the outpouring of the Spirit at the beginning of this age came the promise that the prophetic ministry would not be limited to a few, but diffused through the whole body of Christ. The Church has always experienced spiritual decline when its preaching has lost the prophetic fire. In the Early Church the prophetic element in the preaching was conspicuous.

Obviously Luke could give us only a small sample of the preaching of those glorious days. Each record is necessarily a condensation of what often may have been a long sermon. Although the preaching of the Early Church leaders did not sound formally structured or compressed into a homiletical mold, it was not disorganized or haphazard. The Spirit of God is not the author of confusion. Neither is He the author of slovenly preaching habits, which certainly confuse more than enlighten.

Peter at Pentecost

Naturally Peter's sermon at Pentecost was extemporaneous. The anointing of the Spirit, however, gave it depth and order. It was necessary that he first answer the questions and accusations of the crowd. He did not spend long doing this; then he quickly referred to the Old Testament Scriptures. Those devout Jews were familiar with Joel's prophecy. Peter cried, "You're seeing it fulfilled before your eyes!" (See Acts 2:16-21.)

Having established a scriptural foundation, Peter moved quickly to his main point. The fulfillment of this prophecy had awaited the redemptive work of the Messiah, whom he boldly declared is Jesus.

The apostle reminded his audience of the miracles Jesus had wrought among them. They were His divine credentials, but the answer of the nation had been crucifixion instead of worship. Peter made no attempt to smooth over their crime. They were "wicked hands" that had killed the Messiah (2:23).

Again Peter went to the Scriptures, quoting from the Psalms to prove both the death and resurrection of Jesus were foretold by God. Preachers like to build their sermons to a spine-tingling climax. Such a moment was surely reached in Peter's message when he shouted: "This Jesus hath God raised up, whereof we all are witnesses" (2:32).

But where is Jesus now? "By the right hand of God exalted" (v. 33). What about this strange thing that had just taken place? If Joel prophesied it, who was responsible for bringing it to pass? "Having received of the Father the promise of the Holy Ghost, he hath shed forth this, which ye now see and hear."

Then the summary: "Therefore let all the house of Israel know assuredly, that God hath made that same Jesus, whom ye have crucified, both Lord and Christ" (2:36). The Spirit did His convicting work: "They were pricked in their heart." It was not superficial, for it was followed by the cry, "Men and brethren, what shall we do?"

The first word of Peter's answer was, "Repent." Their repentance and acceptance of Jesus must be openly declared by their baptism in water. Peter assured them two things would result: (1) their sins would be forgiven; and (2) they would receive the gift of the Holy Spirit. This promise, he said, is for everyone who accepts Jesus Christ throughout the Church Age.

Before he gave his altar call Peter made it clear he was not inviting the people to an easy path. They lived in an "untoward generation"—warped and perverse. They must save themselves from it. If anyone imagines such plain preaching will drive people away, let him read verse 41: "Then they that gladly received his word were baptized: and the same day there were added unto them about three thousand souls."

Peter at the Temple Gate

The occasion for this sermon was a miracle (3:1-11). To his Jewish audience Peter declared that it was the God of their great ancestors, Abraham, Isaac, and Jacob, who raised Jesus from the dead. Then he shot the fiery dart of accusation: Their hands were covered, he said, with the blood of God's Son. But after they killed Him, God raised Him up (3:14, 15).

If the people doubted Jesus is alive they needed only to look at the man who had just been healed. "His name, through faith in his name, hath made this man strong," Peter testified. "And now, brethren, I wot that through ignorance ye did it, as did also your rulers" (3:16, 17). It was all foretold by God through the prophets, he assured them.

"Repent ye therefore. . . ." This would not only bring forgiveness of their sins but also "times of refreshing . . . from the presence of the Lord." Peter also introduced the truth of Christ's return.

Again the apostle showed his reliance on the Word, quoting Moses and reminding his hearers they were the descendants of Abraham and the prophets who had foretold the ministry of Jesus. He referred them to their Bible, the Old Testament. He was determined to impress on them that the message of Christ had the backing of the Scriptures.

Peter at Caesarea

Was Peter the only apostle who preached? Indeed

not. It is not surprising, though, that we hear so much from him in the early days of the Church. His simple but forceful ministry was just what was needed to blaze the Church's first trails in a world that had said a violent "No" to the Saviour.

The circumstances of Peter's message at Caesarea were different. Peter stood in a Gentile's house, still bewildered that he was there. His first words were probably spoken to himself as much as to his audience: "Of a truth I perceive that God is no respecter of persons" (10:34).

Apparently those people were familiar with the ministry of John the Baptist. Peter referred to it, assuring his audience that John was God's messenger who had come to introduce Jesus. How beautifully he summed up the Saviour's earthly ministry: "How God anointed Jesus of Nazareth with the Holy Ghost and with power: who went about doing good, and healing all that were oppressed of the devil; for God was with him" (10:38).

Peter was anxious for the Gentiles to know he was not giving them second-hand information. He and his companions were eyewitnesses of everything Jesus did during His public ministry. Above all, they ate and drank with Him after He rose from the dead. Peter introduced the truth of Christ's future role as Judge. Again he asserted that the Old Testament bears witness to Jesus, and assured his listeners of the forgiveness of their sins through Him.

Peter didn't finish this message quite like the others. The Spirit interrupted him, and he suddenly heard the people speaking with tongues. They had accepted Jesus and been filled with the Spirit almost simultaneously. Peter, the devout Jew, did not try to argue with God. He quickly conducted a water baptismal service (10:44-48). These Gentiles were now his brothers and sisters in Christ. They invited him to stay and tell them more, and I have no doubt that he accepted.

Paul at Antioch in Pisidia

This sermon is unusual because it was preached in a Jewish synagogue. After the usual ritual the officials invited their guests to speak. Paul was right at home. His life had been centered in the synagogue and the teachings of the Old Testament. Graciously he addressed the congregation, "Men of Israel, and ye that fear God" (13:16).

Paul wisely began on familiar ground. He reminded the people of a thrilling episode in their nation's history. Their ancestors had been slaves in Egypt. When their suffering had become unbearable God delivered them "with a high arm" ("uplifted arm," *NASB*). His audience listened intently. They never wearied of that story. Every year at Passover they celebrated it. They taught it to their children, who taught it to theirs. It made every one of them proud he was a Jew.

Paul did not omit the disobedience of Israel that resulted in their 40 years' wandering. Before he finished he had made it clear that the Jewish nation had failed God again by refusing to accept His Son.

Carefully and methodically Paul, with his profound knowledge of the Scriptures, brought his listeners through the years of Israel's history (13:19-22). He referred to the dark era of the Judges. He spoke of the day the people had rejected God as king and insisted on an earthly ruler. In His mercy God had granted their demands. And when the first king failed, God brought David to the throne.

Now Paul's audience really came to life. David

was their great hero. The Messiah would come from his lineage. The apostle seized on that very hope to proclaim it had already happened! God had raised up a Saviour of the seed of David—His name is Jesus!

Paul emphasized the witness of John the Baptist to Christ. Still addressing the people as "men and brethren," he focused on the rejection of Jesus by the Jewish religious leaders. They had heard the "prophets . . . read every sabbath day," but were ignorant of their real message (13:27).

Paul's indictment was clear. The Jewish hierarchy had found no real basis for demanding Jesus' death, but they did it anyway. They did not know they were fulfilling the Scriptures. Neither did they dream they had not heard the last of Jesus when they took His dead body from the cross. But God had the last word. He raised His Son from the dead (v. 30).

By now Paul's audience must have been breathless. They had followed him in his journey through Hebrew history. But then he dropped his bombshell. Paul turned to the Psalms and piled Scripture upon Scripture until the evidence was overwhelming. Although rejected by His own people, Jesus is the promised Messiah. He conquered death and now reigns at God's right hand.

Paul assured the people their sins could be forgiven through Jesus. And he quickly followed with a warning of the consequences of rejecting God's offer of salvation (13:40, 41).

The service seemed to end quietly. There can be little doubt that most members of the congregation were dumbfounded. Some may have been almost in a state of shock. There were Gentiles in the congregation who asked Paul to remain, and many of the Jews joined them.

Paul on Mars' Hill

Paul preached in strange places. He made a brief stop in Athens; waiting for Silas and Timothy to meet him. The slavery of the Athenians to idolatry stirred him to the depths of his being. First he preached in the synagogue, then in the *agora*—the marketplace or town square.

This was a very different crowd. There were philosophers, as well as many who simply enjoyed hearing and telling every new thing they heard. The Athenians had a thirst for knowledge, and the *agora* was always a busy place where all kinds of ideas were exchanged.

Paul made no attempt to dilute his message in this cultural center. He preached Jesus and the Resurrection. Some called him a babbler. Others said he was proclaiming strange gods.

The *agora* was a noisy place. Paul gladly went with a group to the Areopagus (Mars' Hill) where there could be a quieter discussion. He had brought a "new doctrine" to town, and they wanted to know more about it.

The King James Version translates Paul's opening remark: "I perceive that in all things ye are too superstitious" (17:22). A better rendering is: "I observe that you are very religious in all respects" *(NASB)*. Paul used the inscription on one of their altars as the subject of his sermon: "The Unknown God." "He is the one I represent," he announced. "He may be unknown to you, but not to me."

The God Paul preached about at Athens is the Creator of the universe. He needs no earthly temple. He is the Giver of life. He created men to worship Him.

Paul quoted one of the Athenians' own poets who

said, "We are [God's] offspring." "If this is true," the apostle said, "we should not imagine the One from whom we have sprung is made of metal or stone." Paul's approach was different from the way he preached in the synagogues, but he had the same message.

Like Peter, Paul never soft-pedaled the doctrine of repentance. He warned his cultured audience that if they did not repent they would face Christ at the Judgment. That judgment is assured because the Judge has been raised from the dead.

Undoubtedly Paul knew some would mock his message of the Resurrection, but this did not keep him from proclaiming it. They did mock. Some simply suggested that Paul come back again.

There is no indication Paul returned to Mars' Hill. His listeners had their opportunity, and most of them rejected it. However, there were a few who believed. God's Word did not return to Him void. Athens had heard the message, and Christ now had disciples there (17:34).

There was not the violent reaction in Athens that Paul had so often encountered. His listeners considered themselves sophisticated enough to hear every point of view. Paul's message was simply another philosophy for them to mull over in their minds—so they reasoned. They were too hardened in their smug, self-satisfied ways to even become angry.

Peter and Paul were as different as day and night in temperament and background. Paul's intellectual credentials were formidable. He was a rabbi; Peter was a fisherman. Yet one grand theme dominated the preaching of both: Jesus Christ, crucified and risen from the dead, is the world's only Saviour.